Praise for *Seven Cups of Consciousness*

"Aleya Dao cuts to the core of soul work with both simplicity and complexity: simplicity in how she delivers, and complexity in how she invites us to let go of what we have known. *Seven Cups of Consciousness* is highly recommended for deepening consciousness and connecting into greater divinity and wholeness."

— Simran Singh, creator of *11:11* magazine and *11:11* talk radio and author of *Conversations with the Universe*

"When truth speaks, you just know it. That's how you'll feel reading Aleya Dao's *Seven Cups of Consciousness*. Each 'cup' is an awakening to a greater aspect of who you really are and the magnificence of your divine self. Journey with Aleya and witness the perspective of your physical life shifting to a greater understanding of purpose and wondrous adventure."

— Jean Slatter, author of *Hiring the Heavens*

"Aleya Dao's new book, *Seven Cups of Consciousness*, is a refreshing new approach that teaches you how to use her techniques to create change in your day-to-day life. Using stories to illustrate not only Dao's own success but her clients' experiences, this book is easy, fun, and enlightening to read."

— Sonia Choquette, *New York Times*–bestselling author of *The Answer Is Simple*

"*Seven Cups of Consciousness* is a book that inspires and empowers. Aleya Dao takes a unique approach, explaining how to utilize the resources in other dimensions in a way that all readers can grasp. If you are at all interested in changing your life using an alternative, higher-dimensional approach, this is a must-read."

— Lynn Andrews, *New York Times*–bestselling author of
the Medicine Woman series

SEVEN CUPS *of* Consciousness

Also by Aleya Dao

Sound Healing Albums

Awaken
by Aleya Dao and Barry Goldstein

In Stillness
by Aleya Dao, George Friedenthal,
and Robinson Eikenberry

Light Body Sound Healing
by Aleya Dao

Om-ing with Whales
by Aleya Dao and the Humpback Whales

Sound Medicine
by Aleya Dao

SEVEN CUPS *of* Consciousness

*Change Your Life by Connecting to
the Higher Realms*

Aleya Dao

New World Library
Novato, California

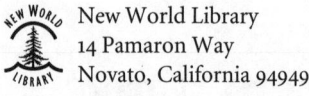

New World Library
14 Pamaron Way
Novato, California 94949

The material in this book is intended for education. It is not meant to take the place of diagnosis and treatment by a qualified medical practitioner or therapist. No guarantee of the effects of using the recommendations can be given, nor liability taken. All names and genders in this book have been changed to protect privacy.

"Cups of Consciousness" is a registered trademark of Aleya Dao.

Text design by Tona Pearce Myers

Library of Congress Cataloging-in-Publication Data
Dao, Aleya, date.
  Seven cups of consciousness : change your life by connecting to the higher realms / Aleya Dao.
    pages cm
  ISBN 978-1-60868-332-1 (pbk. : alk. paper) — ISBN 978-1-60868-333-8 (ebook)
  1. Spirituality. 2. Consciousness—Miscellanea. I. Title.
  BF1999.D265 2015
  131—dc23   2015016217

First printing, September 2015
ISBN 978-1-60868-332-1
Printed in the USA on 100% postconsumer-waste recycled paper

 New World Library is proud to be a Gold Certified Environmentally Responsible Publisher. Publisher certification awarded by Green Press Initiative. www.greenpressinitiative.org

10   9   8   7   6   5   4   3   2   1

This book is dedicated to all my clients.
Thank you for inviting me into your inner sacred space.
It has been a profound honor and privilege
to serve, assist, and guide you.

Contents

Introduction

*I*magine a life filled with happiness, connection, and purpose. Just think: You are able to connect with the divine and perfect aspect of yourself. You feel protected and guided by a loving angelic presence. You use every challenge to grow stronger and to access a higher consciousness. You are healthy and filled with self-love. Deep inside, you feel creative, passionate, and joyful — and all of that is reflected into your life.

Wouldn't that be lovely?

Well, it is possible, and I am here to show you how. The basic idea is that all your work is done at a level higher than your physical reality. There are aspects of you that exist in higher dimensions, at the spiritual level. I call these parts of you your energy self or your Higher Self.

I have created a step-by-step process to help you gain access to your energy self and the energetic resources it controls. As you develop these tools, your consciousness will evolve, your challenges will transform, and a deep inner peace and empowerment will bloom.

You will learn that your real power comes from within and from beyond. When you explore your inner realms, along with the higher dimensions, your life will start to change in amazing ways.

For many years I looked for fulfillment externally. My life was a half-empty cold cup of coffee. I felt a deep sense of emptiness, even though everything on the outside looked "perfect." I was living in a beautiful mountain town. I had a thriving acupuncture practice. I was healthy, had great friends, and was single and dating, yet this full life was not enough. I yearned for an inner change, wanting something, anything, that would fill my emptiness.

I chased numerous spiritual teachings, hoping that each one would give me the answer. I longed for an enlightenment moment that would miraculously transform my life into one of bliss and joy. But nothing could have prepared me for what was to come.

In the middle of a sound healing session, I was hit by the cosmic two-by-four. I had an awakening. In less than thirty seconds, my consciousness radically altered. A bright light enveloped me. My awareness shifted into a higher realm, and I felt an exquisite vibration of love, as I saw the world surrounded by loving, compassionate beings. Waves of light coursed through me, filling me with new ideas, perspectives, memories, and pearls of wisdom. In every fiber of my being, I could feel and see a multidimensional reality.

I started to see the world through new eyes. It was like getting X-ray glasses. I could feel a deep interconnectedness and purpose behind everything. The fabric of the world looked like an exquisite pattern of love and light, instead of a dark, shadowy, and challenging place. I understood the reason behind every action, and I had a profound awareness of what needs and lessons were being addressed by other people's behavior. This greater awareness was simultaneously overwhelming, empowering, and comforting.

You would think that having a deep inner knowing of connection and peace would make life a cakewalk. I wish. Often the opposite is true. Life gets real, very quickly.

As you awaken, you will become more sensitive. This sensitivity will become your greatest strength and your greatest challenge. You will need tools to protect this new level of awareness. You will also need discernment, empowerment, and courage.

As you become more sensitive, you may feel other people's feelings, hear angelic beings and guides, hear or know the thoughts of others, see beings of light and dark, and maybe even see the future of your life and of others'. These experiences may be both comforting and frightening.

You might also experience a conflicting sense of connection and deep loneliness. Old relationships could fall away. You could even find yourself living in a new place, driving a new car, wearing new clothes, and maybe even taking a new name.

Less than six months after my enlightenment experience, I had experienced all the above, and more. My entire life had changed in the blink of an eye. I had to let go of the old and move into the new. I slowly discovered the tools to help me navigate the unknown waters with ease and eventually with grace. I was my very own guinea pig, and my life was the lab. I learned how to discern the difference between my thoughts and feelings and the thoughts and feelings of others. I learned how to hold appropriate boundaries, meet my needs internally, and take responsibility for my inner and outer reality. I met my beloved partner, found a beautiful home, and created a bountiful livelihood.

I am not saying it was easy. I fell down a lot, had my heart broken a few times, spent way more money than I had in my bank account, moved seven times, got sick, got healthy, lost friends, and made new ones. My learning curve was steep and involved many tears, laughs, and thinking I was insane for brief moments of time. Fortunately, I had guidance through the entire process of integrating a higher consciousness.

Through trial and error, and with the help of my angelic guides (beings of love and light who exist in a higher dimension), I have developed seven concepts that have proved useful to my clients, my students, and myself. When understood, practiced, and mastered, these concepts can help you create the life you yearn for, one of abundance, balance, connection, and empowerment. When you take the conscious, slow, gentle path, you will save time, money, relationships, and your general sanity. This book will give you the tools to do just that.

THE SEVEN CUPS OF CONSCIOUSNESS

After fourteen years of practice and teaching, I have distilled these concepts into what I call the Cups of Consciousness.

In 2009 I started recording and delivering daily audio meditations and monthly webinars that pull from these concepts. These meditations quickly became known as the Cups of Consciousness because, just as a cup of coffee or tea can help you wake up in the morning, the meditations and concepts trigger a gradual awakening to higher levels of consciousness.

These Cups of Consciousness have helped thousands of people from all over the world find peace and joy. My clients, subscribers, and students have repeatedly asked me to reduce these concepts that are infused into the daily Cups of Consciousness meditations and the online Tall Cups of Consciousness webinars into a book. The book you hold in your hands is the result.

In it you will learn about these seven fundamental concepts, each of which blends in with and builds on all the others. In each chapter I explain a cup and share a story about how I discovered and refined the cup with my clients and myself. I share specific protocols, which are energetic practices, and point you to the audio meditations that will help you embody the consciousness of each cup. As you master each cup, you will find your life becoming more fulfilling, connected, and joyful.

The seven cups are simple statements of truth:

First Cup: You Live in a Multidimensional Reality.
Second Cup: You Are Never Alone.
Third Cup: You Can Change Your Inner World.
Fourth Cup: Your Challenges Can Help You Grow.
Fifth Cup: Your Body Is a Nature Spirit.
Sixth Cup: Your Soul Has Wisdom and Inner Gifts.
Seventh Cup: You Are Perfect.

Combining these concepts can help you form a big picture of reality that can dramatically transform your life. If you sip from just one of these cups, however, it can help you find greater peace and empowerment.

If some of the cups do not resonate with you, put them aside. You can always come back to them — or not. Your life will change positively whether you master just one or all seven of the cups.

The Recipe: Protocols

Each cup comes with particular energetic exercises that I refer to as protocols. Each step within a protocol walks your energy self through a process that helps you release old patterns and access a higher consciousness. The protocols are directed at the energetic aspect of you, not your mind. When you digest the information at the level of your energetic self, your mind will understand the concepts much more quickly.

If you are religiously inclined, you might consider these protocols to be prayers. If you are psychologically oriented, you may consider them a form of cognitive behavioral therapy. Regardless of how you label them, these protocols have proved to be very powerful at shifting deep, core issues. They are not meant to take the place of therapy, however; rather, they are a distilled form of spiritual practice.

Though the concepts appear elegant in their simplicity, at their core they are complex. Be patient. You should not realistically expect dramatic changes overnight. However, it could happen. Practice the concepts, and the changes will come.

Audio Meditations

Every chapter provides audio meditations that will help you experience the concepts and protocols more profoundly. You can also listen to the meditations that correlate to each cup. You will want to experience the meditation after reading the chapter to get the full experience of the concept and protocol. Go to www.cups ofconsciousness.com/meditations to listen to the audio meditations and to access all the online material.

You can listen to these meditations as many times as you like. I recommend listening to one or two meditations and then letting the work integrate. If you listen to ten different meditations in one sitting, you might get a headache or feel weird. It's analogous to eating too much in one sitting. Think of them as meditation medication. The audio meditations and protocols can be powerful, so go slowly and let your desires and intuition guide you. They will pulse you into right action with the work.

A Brief Overview of the Seven Cups

Using the seven cups can give you the power to shift yourself. Over time, these inner shifts will be reflected in your life. You will gain a level of control that is healthy and empowering.

You are perfect. A light flows inside you that is your essence. Your inner light is beautiful and whole. Your primary job is to love the light inside you and model it in the world. You have spent lifetimes creating and refining very particular qualities inside you, such as peace, empowerment, clarity, or love. These qualities, which I perceive as energetic vibrations, are your Soul's wisdom, inner gifts, and mastery. When you use your wisdom and inner gifts, your life becomes abundant and supported.

You are never alone. You have angelic guides and a Team, which exist in other dimensions. They are here to help and protect you. Your angelic Team members surround your Higher Self and can be a great source of support and protection. Your Team has been with you since the time of your birth; as a child you may have thought of them as your imaginary friends. Your Team members are always with you, whereas your guides come and go, depending on your needs. Using your angelic resources can assist you in powerful ways.

You live in a world of multiple dimensions. The physical realm is only one of many. You are a multidimensional being expressing yourself in multiple dimensions. The physical world is only one part of your reality. Reach beyond the limited physical experience. Tap into and use the energetic aspect of yourself.

Your human body is from Earth. It is a nature spirit that has its own unique consciousness and is in a process of spiritual evolution, as are you. It is the vehicle you ride in. You are not your body. When you are in harmony with your body, your ride will be far less bumpy.

Your internal reality creates your outer world. What you focus on is what you create. Every challenge is an opportunity for you to grow, learn, evolve, and embody a higher, more connected, and empowered level of consciousness.

The Teachings

I think of my teachings as a restatement of ancient wisdom. Religious and spiritual traditions simply have different ways of expressing these same concepts.

Buddhism teaches the concept that we are all one. If you use the Seventh Cup and connect with your inner river of light, you tap into oneness, which is essentially the God-self. You are an expression of the God energy.

Many Christians believe in the Holy Trinity: the Father, Son, and Holy Ghost. In discussing the seven cups, I refer to your Soul/essence, your body, and the Team as the sacred trinity.

There is an ancient saying, "When two or more are gathered in the name of the nameless one (the divine, Oneness, God), manifestation becomes evident." When you, your body, and your Team all align to a particular intention, manifestation occurs.

I never ask anyone to accept my wisdom on faith. You have to see for yourself the power of the Cups of Consciousness. The best teacher is you. All seven cups will help you create a spiritual practice. As with all spiritual practices, practice, test, and use discernment about what works and doesn't work for you.

A much deeper journey is embedded in each cup that gently unfolds as you embody this higher consciousness. As you read the following pages, you will pick up information from the words I have written. In addition, you will become open to information flowing from a higher spiritual level. This flow will be almost outside your consciousness. To access it, simply invite your energetic self to receive this higher information. Ask your energy self to extract what you need, then digest and integrate the information in a way that serves you. Your mind will understand and "get it" once your energy self has integrated the information.

No matter what happens, I promise you an interesting read. The catch, of course, is enlightenment — the gentle, easy way. Read on and awaken more deeply as you sip from the Cups of Consciousness.

FIRST CUP

You Live in a Multidimensional Reality

> **You are a multidimensional being expressing yourself in multiple realms.**

*T*he world you live in is made up of multiple dimensions. The physical dimension is just one floor of a multistory building. Each floor or dimension holds different energies and levels of consciousness.

The physical dimension contains solid objects, a linear time line, finite resources, and limited space. You can only accomplish a certain amount in a day, depending on your energy level, the amount of time you have, and the resources available to you. It is a finite experience.

The nonphysical dimensions are more etheric realities. Time is not linear, space is infinite, and resources are endless. For example, when you dream, a few seconds may seem like several hours. During a meditation, you may grasp a concept in seconds that might otherwise take years of study to fully comprehend. When you use your imagination or fantasize, you are accessing different dimensions that contain different layers of information and perspectives.

Let's take a quick dimensional trip. Imagine standing in the lobby of a hotel. You step into a glass elevator and press the button for the sixth floor. As you ascend and look down at the lobby, you have a different vantage point. You see things that you could not see before. When you arrive on the sixth floor, you are able to access information that would have been otherwise unavailable. Once you have gathered all the information you need, you travel back down to the lobby. When you use your energetic glass elevator, you may find yourself traveling faster than light and receiving profound wisdom. You will see your challenges from a different angle. You will come up with solutions and receive new insights.

The information you access can be viewed as physiological (simply a function of the human brain), as spiritual (a connection to God), or as an energetic multidimensional reality, depending on how you view the nature of the Universe.

The key lies in your ability to focus on your inner world, using your imagination and intent as a way to connect to other dimensions. When you close your eyes and focus on your breath, you take your awareness off your outer physical life and move into an inner dimensional one. This shift in awareness opens you up to a multidimensional reality.

As you sip from this First Cup, I will share with you how to stay in your glass elevator and safely travel from the physical dimension up into the higher dimensions. You will learn how to receive information from these higher realms in a way that empowers you and helps you change your life.

Your Multidimensional Reality

Let's take a moment to explore some of the energetic facets that make up your multidimensional reality.

Divine Line

Inside you flows an energetic river of light that I call the divine line. It is energetically attached to the front of your spine. Imagine your divine line as a column, a tube, or your inner glass elevator shaft. The light that flows in your divine line is your essence, the aspect of you that is divine and perfect. You are just a beam of light. Isn't that refreshing? All you need to do is love the light that flows in your divine line. That should be much easier than loving your belief systems, your behavior, your consciousness, and any issues you might have.

The more you hold your awareness in your divine line, the easier your life becomes. If you hold your awareness outside your divine line, you will experience disconnection, loneliness, and a fear of abandonment. When you take a deep breath and pull yourself into your divine line, you will perceive a greater sense of connection and safety.

Higher Self

Your Higher Self is the aspect of you that is expressed in a higher dimension. When you travel up your divine line, you are able to connect with your Higher Self, which has access to your energetic fields. Think of it as the aspect of you that is hanging out on the higher floors and has the bird's-eye view.

Divine Spark

You also express yourself in the divine Source. Source is known in many religions as God or the place where we are all One. From my perspective, God is not an omniscient being or person. Instead, God or Source is the essential consciousness that creates life and being-ness in this Universe. Each of us is an aspect of Source. I call this aspect your divine spark; it is your God-self. Your spark creates a reflection of light that creates your divine line. You are just a beam of light expressing and radiating from Source. How lovely.

Divine Cosmic Loop

You have another energetic aspect that I call your divine cosmic loop. Your divine spark creates your divine line, which loops. Imagine light flowing from your divine spark in the heart of Source, down through the top of your head, down the front of your spine, out your base chakra, and into the heart of Earth. It then loops back up to your divine spark in the heart of Source. When you hold your awareness in your divine cosmic loop, you will feel a greater sense of freedom, power, and connection.

Body Deva

Your body has its own consciousness, which I call the body deva. I think of the body deva as a nature spirit and as an aspect of Earth. Your body deva has its own divine line, just like you do. While your divine line runs along the front of your spine, your body deva's divine line runs through the spine, more specifically within and around the spinal cord. It flows out the base of the spine, into the heart of Earth. Earth is also a conscious, evolving being. She too has a divine spark in the heart of Source that creates her own divine cosmic loop. Your body deva's divine line is connected to the cosmic loop of Earth.

Energy Fields and Chakras

As your divine line flows up and down the front of the spine, and your body deva's divine line flows through the spine, energy passes back and forth between these two lines. This exchange of energy and information creates the energy centers known as chakras, which in turn create your energy fields.

Your energy fields are another energetic aspect of you. Your Higher Self uses your energy fields to receive information, shift energy, and connect with your body deva and your Team.

Your Higher Self is far wiser than your mind. It carries your Soul's wisdom from all your lifetimes. This energetic part of you does all your heavy lifting in the higher realms. The more you use your Higher Self, the faster and stronger your shifts will be.

Your Team and Guides

You are not alone. You have both guides and a Team of angelic beings who surround and support you. Your Team members are Souls who are living in a higher dimension and have agreed to support you. You may perceive them as male or female or as a group. Your Team members surround you 24/7, never leaving you. Your guides appear and support you depending on your needs. Your guides are usually more evolved than you and your Team. They may consist of archangels, saints, or Ascended Masters, all of whom are highly evolved beings. Your guides and Team are here to help you. All you need to do is ask.

The Higher Self, divine lines, divine spark, divine cosmic loop, chakras, energetic fields, Team, and guides are all expressed in nonphysical dimensions. You can use these dimensional aspects as resources to help you evolve your consciousness, manifest your intentions, and transform your challenges.

Since an image is worth a thousand words, you can go online to see the images I created that depict these energetic aspects: www.cupsofconsciousness/meditations.

The Cosmic Two-by-Four

During my first enlightenment experience in 2001, I was engulfed in a multidimensional reality, which felt just as real as the physical world. It was an amazing, overwhelming, clarifying experience that took me years to fully comprehend and integrate.

Your first experience of a multidimensional reality may be just as mind-blowing. Any time your perception of reality radically shifts in a positive way, it is a moment of enlightenment. You may have many mini-moments of enlightenment in your life, or you may have one big one. To give you a taste of what a "big one" feels like, I will share mine in more detail.

My awakening moment came while I was receiving a sound healing session. As Mary McLaughlin's "Bring the Peace" pulsed through the sound table, and I took a deep breath, my consciousness abruptly altered.

My awareness instantly shifted from the physical realm into a higher realm. A white light flashed over me, and I found myself standing on a platform of light looking down at the planet. I felt an exquisite vibration of love. I saw thousands of light-beings full of love and compassion surrounding Earth. Millions of lines of light encircled the planet, creating spheres and grids that held uncountable numbers of vibrations and consciousnesses.

I felt peaceful, warm, safe, and connected to this exquisite fabric of love. There was a profound sense of support and strength inside me. I had clarity and a deep understanding about the nature and purpose of life that reached far beyond the simple knowing of my mind.

I felt a group of light-beings around me, and a surge of energy pushed me off my platform of light. I instinctively curled into a tight ball as I accelerated down a tunnel. The music became louder, and I felt myself passing through thick blankets of light, the energetic veils that separate the dimensions.

I became aware of my body and felt a current of energy rushing down the back of my neck and down the front of my spine. I could feel a river of light flowing through the top of my head, down the front of my spine, through the center of Earth, and looping up behind me into the heart of Source, where my divine spark resides. I could feel and hear a group of energetic beings around me. I would later refer to this river of light as my divine line, and the angelic ones as my Team.

I felt my body tingling and radiating with energy. I could literally feel the light emanating from my fingertips. My awareness of the other realms activated. I felt the exquisite vibration of love encompassing everything. I had a deep inner knowing of my own essence and of my journey that extended far beyond my earthly years. All that I had known quietly faded away and a deep peace, connection, and inner knowing of who I truly am came into being. From that moment on, I was aware.

Many mystics have talked about this experience as an *awakening* or as *enlightenment,* and I can see why. I literally awakened to a new reality. Everything was different. I could see through the veils, the energetic curtains that separate the dimensions. I perceived swirls of color, light, and sound representing subtle energies. Information flowed to me via channels that had just opened up for me. I could see and understand a new conception of reality.

I slowly got off the table and instantly felt dizzy. I sat down for a moment and collected myself before I quietly thanked the practitioner and headed for the door. As I stood outside, taking deep breaths of cold air, I felt my Team surround me. I got in my car, and heard them say: "Now drive."

I thought to myself, "Sure, no problem. I just shifted my entire reality. I have had a massive spiritual awakening, and I am now able to perceive multiple dimensions simultaneously. My body is tingling and shaking with energy. And they want me to drive?" I made it two blocks before I had to pull over and walk the short distance home.

That night as I lay in bed vibrating, I thought about my new reality. I could feel a river of light inside me. I could feel how the river is connected to Source. I could perceive other realms and beings in other realms. I could hear other people's thoughts and feel their feelings. If I had not been an alternative medicine practitioner and a doctor of Oriental Medicine, I might have thought I was experiencing a psychotic break. Fortunately, I had read about all the potential symptoms of an enlightenment experience.

Of course, it's one thing to read about these experiences, but to actually have them…? Well, there is no comparison. Your journey is yours, and yours alone. Whatever you have read in a book (even this one) cannot completely prepare you for a major shift in consciousness. But it can help remove the fear of having totally lost it.

DEVELOPING YOUR ENERGETIC SENSES

Being aware of and feeling the energy in the other dimensions is different from feeling and being aware of energy in the physical dimension. It is not something you can tangibly see with your eyes, touch with your hands, smell with your nose, or hear with your ears. The energy in the other realms is subtle. It may feel like little wisps of energetic wind, a flash of light, a tingle on your arm, a quick high-pitched ringing in your ears, a weird swirling sensation in your head.

Your body's five senses give you information about the physical dimension. In addition to your five physical senses, you have five energetic senses. When you develop your energetic senses, you will be able to perceive other dimensions.

The easiest way to develop your energetic senses is to identify your strongest physical sense. When you talk, do you describe things by the way they look, sound, feel, smell, or taste? Are you more sensitive to light, sounds, smells, taste, or touch? When you determine your strongest physical sense, you can focus on strengthening and opening this sense at an energetic level.

Imagine having energetically sensitive eyes, ears, nose, mouth, or hands. Think of these energetic senses as your sixth sense. They pick up information in dimensions other than the physical. *Clairsentience* is energetically feeling, also know as empathic sensitivity. *Clairvoyance* is using your energetic eyes, also known as your third eye. Hearing energetically is called *clairaudience*. *Clairgnosis* is clear knowing. The ability to energetically taste is *clairgustance*. And having an energetically awakened nose is *clairalience*. Everyone has the ability to energetically feel, hear, see, smell, and taste. You may have already developed a few of your five energetic senses.

When you are just beginning, I recommend using your imagination. Imagining your energetic senses puts them into your conscious awareness, where you can pay better attention to them. The sensations are so subtle that, with all the noise of life, they can be easy to miss.

The more you use your Higher Self, imagination, and intent, the more you will develop multidimensional awareness. The energetic protocols and meditations in this book will also help you develop your energetic senses. I recommend doing this slowly and carefully. It can be intense if you go too quickly.

GET IN YOUR DIVINE LINE

Before you jump into pumping up your five energetic senses, I recommend first learning how to connect with your divine line. My expanded awareness of other dimensions was overwhelming; I needed to find a place where I could go that would be quiet, safe, peaceful, and calm. That place was in the inner waterfall of light: my divine line. You will need a place of refuge as well.

I learned the importance of connecting with my divine line from my angelic Team. One night I was having a hard time sleeping, which was not unusual, since sleep was hard to come by those first few years after my enlightenment experience. As I gazed up through the skylight at the starry sky, I felt the familiar presence of my Team. A soft shimmering vibration radiated around me. I felt a swirling in my head that made me dizzy as I received the energetic information. (I quickly learned that the fastest and easiest way to receive energetic information was to relax, close my eyes, let go of my need to know what the information was, and just feel the energy coming from my Higher Self.)

I felt my Team members come closer and heard their gentle, loving words, inviting me to take a deep breath in. As I relaxed, they pointed to the light flowing up and down the front of my spine. My Team said, "This is your divine line. Hold as much of your awareness as possible here. Connecting with your divine line is the safest way to travel to higher dimensions."

With each inhale I pulled myself more and more deeply into my divine line. After a few minutes, I felt a warm flow of energy gently pulsing up and down the front of my spine. I could see a beautiful, pure light flowing in this column, and a sense of peace and calm enveloped me. I felt myself standing in an exquisite shaft of light.

As I held my awareness on my divine line, my Team instructed me to firmly attach my divine line, which was bubbling off, to the front of my spine. I used my breath and asked my Higher Self to use my energy fields to firmly attach my divine line to the front of my spine.

If your divine line is not fully attached to the front of your spine it will negatively affect your chakras, your ability to be grounded, and your connection to your body. Imagine driving your car while simultaneously holding yourself off the driver's seat. If you have resistance about being in a human body, your divine line will not be firmly attached to the front of your spine and may bubble off, as mine did initially. This resistance makes for a bumpy ride.

You can use your breath, intention, and imagination to energetically glue, Velcro, clip, or button your divine line to the front of your spine. Use whatever energetic mechanism you wish to attach yourself to the front of the spine, as long as it feels comfortable and empowering.

The more awareness you hold in your divine line, the bigger and brighter it will become. In this inner river, you are perfect.

HOLDING YOUR AWARENESS IN YOUR DIVINE LINE

Let's practice connecting to your divine line using your imagination and your intent. Imagine a river of light flowing from the top of your head, down the front of your spine, and out your base chakra, which is at the base of your spine. Take a deep breath. As you breathe in, imagine pulling yourself into this river of light. Imagine standing in the middle of a gentle waterfall of light. Nestle into the flow, and imagine snuggling up to the front of your spine. Take another breath, and perceive from inside this column of light. Explore the quality of the light that flows in this inner river. Does it feel soothing, empowering, and safe? The stronger your connection to your river of light, the more empowered, connected, safe, and controlled your energetic ascent will be.

When you use a specific protocol as opposed to your imagination, the impact is even greater. Below is the specific protocol to help you connect with your divine line. All protocols are designed to help your Higher Self shift your energy in the higher realms.

CONNECTING TO YOUR DIVINE LINE

Read the following steps either silently or out loud:

"I ask my Higher Self to work with my energetic fields to energetically locate my divine line." Take a breath. Wait. Hold awareness that your Higher Self is doing the work in a higher realm.

"I ask my Higher Self to work with my energetic fields to pull all my awareness off of everyone and everything and to bring it back to my divine line. I ask my Higher Self to firmly attach my divine line to the front of my spine."

Take a deep breath, and relax. Close your eyes, and imagine standing in a beautiful river of light that is flowing up and down the front of your spine.

When you sense that your Higher Self has completed the work, make this final request: *"I invite my Higher Self to work with my energetic fields to update all my reference points and ways of perceiving."*

When you update your reference points, you are essentially resetting your energetic fuel gauge or creating a new baseline.

Allow the energetic aspect of you to do the work in the higher realms. (This is the hard part...wait. Let it happen in the higher realms. Your Higher Self knows how to do this work.)

When you connect with the light that flows in your divine

line, you will feel peaceful, connected, and safe. If you sense energy or colors that are not beautiful to you, that is an indicator that you are still holding your awareness outside your divine line. Push yourself deeper, through the darkness, using your inhale, intent, imagination, and Higher Self. Eventually you will hit a beautiful stream of light. Once you do, you may shed tears of relief. You may even experience a state of awe as you witness your incredible inner beauty.

Feeling the Shift

During or after a protocol you may feel a little shift inside you, or you may not. Either way, some part of you is doing the work. Be patient; this process is subtle in the beginning. The more you practice it, the more obvious it will become. You might notice your body twitching when you take a deep breath. You might feel swirling energy within or around you. Allow it to be subtle.

When I first felt the shifts of energy, it would drop me to my knees. I wanted and needed lots of proof. The energy became very uncomfortable in its obvious presence. Now my head just twitches when the energy shifts. It is still obvious but easier to live with than having my knees buckle.

In the years that followed, my Team continued to remind me about my divine line. Eventually, I learned to hold my awareness more in my divine line than on the external world. This has proved to be a much more peaceful and enjoyable way of being.

Society, family, or friends may have conditioned you to seek connection and happiness externally and to find fulfillment from other people, things, and money. Yet when you fulfill your needs internally instead of externally, you move into greater abundance in all areas of your life. The more you hold your awareness in your divine line, the easier your life will be. You will become less reactive and feel a greater connection to the divine aspect of you.

Your Higher Self

When you are holding your awareness in your divine line and are firmly attached to the front of your spine, you are ready to take a trip up your glass elevator to visit your Higher Self.

As you travel up your divine line, you will become aware of your Higher Self — a multicolored body of light. You may feel more expanded and free when you hold your awareness at this level. You may feel your Higher Self around you or above you. Either one works.

Over the years, I have created several metaphors for referring to the Higher Self. When I work with children, I call their Higher Self their "super self." When I work with individuals in the technology industry, I say that the Higher Self works at the level of the "hard drive." When I work with CEOs, I call it "you on the penthouse floor." Other metaphors for the Higher Self are a soaring eagle with the bird's-eye view or your energetic light-body self sitting on a cloud, maybe with angel wings.

Take a moment to think of a metaphor that works for you. Do you have a Higher Self hard drive? Is your energy self on a penthouse floor? Is it your super self? Maybe your Higher Self is sitting on a cloud. Perhaps the image of the glass elevator resonates. Imagine being on a higher floor with a view. After all, it is the wiser, energetic aspect of you. You may think of a metaphor or technique that is different from the ones I have suggested. Use whatever works for you and feels supportive.

Let's say you use computers a lot and that metaphor works for you. You can use your Higher Self and energy fields the same way you use a computer. Imagine using your mind as a mouse (or a track pad). Double-click on your Higher Self as if it's the icon for your hard drive. Ask your Higher Self to open and run the application of self-love. Let your Higher Self access that program.

With computers, unless you're tech-savvy, you don't know or

really care how the programs work, as long as they do. It's the same thing with your Higher Self. Let it do the work without worrying about the programming and engineering aspects happening in the background. You do not need to figure it all out in your head. Your Higher Self knows how to do the work; it does not involve mental effort.

Another metaphor that might help is to imagine that you just placed your order with the waiter. Now you need to let him or her take your request to the kitchen. Let your Higher Self be the head chef that prepares your order. The more you use your Higher Self, the more effortless your life becomes.

It took me a while to grasp this concept. I soon discovered that if I just thought about what I wanted to have happen instead of asking my Higher Self to make it happen, nothing would occur. I would not feel a shift inside, and nothing in my outer world would change, either. I was a type A person who micromanaged everything around me. I learned quickly that I had to trust my Higher Self and not try to create outcomes by sheer willpower. The more I let go of my need for control, the deeper and faster my life shifted. I had to learn to let my Higher Self do the work. In other words, my mind was not the *doer*; it was the asker.

SHIFTING YOUR ENERGETIC BLUEPRINTS

In the physical world there are many aspects of your reality: relationships, health, finances, and so on. In the higher realms you have energetic blueprints for different aspects of your reality. You have a relationship blueprint, a resource/money blueprint, a body health blueprint, and a passion-creativity-career blueprint: every component of your life has an energetic blueprint or map. When you use your Higher Self to shift the energy within and around you, this process is reflected in your physical world as well.

My first palpable experience of this concept was spurred by

my insatiable desire for an intimate relationship. I was single and very determined to find love. One evening I sat in meditation and asked the question, "What is the first step I need to take to help me manifest a beloved partner?"

I quieted my mind by focusing solely on my breath. I held my awareness in my divine line and firmly attached it to the front of my spine. I imagined traveling up my divine line to my Higher Self and held my awareness in that higher dimension.

As I traveled up my glass elevator shaft to my Higher Self, I saw a realm filled with multiple beams of light. They looked like blueprints, similar to what one would find on the desk of an architect, but in 3-D. I felt a very particular energy radiating from each line. I saw multiple blueprints for every aspect of my life. When all the blueprints were combined, they created a shape that looked like a sphere of light. It was exquisitely beautiful and complex.

Holding my awareness and desire to shift the energy around my intimate relationships — or lack thereof — I asked for assistance from my Team. They instructed me to make my request to my Higher Self, so I asked my Higher Self to locate my relationship blueprint. I sat in stillness and watched that energetic aspect of me locate and connect with that specific blueprint. Once that was done, I asked my Higher Self to infuse and activate the vibrations of love, connection, and passion in my divine line and to infuse these same qualities into my relationship blueprint.

I continued to sit in stillness and trust that my Higher Self was doing this work. I had no idea how my Higher Self was doing it, but it was happening. I could feel the reverberations reflecting down from the higher dimensions. I felt a swirling expansion within and around me.

The more my Higher Self worked, the sleepier I got. My meditation turned into a night of deep sleep. When I awoke the next morning, I felt a deep sense of connection, sweetness, and love. The visions of the night before flooded over me, and I realized that the work I had done with my Higher Self had indeed created a shift within me. I hoped this shift would positively affect my love life...

I got out of bed, threw on my running clothes, stepped out the door, and headed for my favorite trail. As I began my run up the hill, I passed a friend who was coming down. She looked at me and said, "Wow, you look amazing! Are you in love?" I almost laughed out loud, and said, "Not yet." As I continued the ascent, I wondered what my friend had seen in me. Was the little bit of work in a higher realm last night really that noticeable? I did feel different. I was calmer and happier and somehow felt fuller inside.

I stopped on a little plateau halfway up the trail and heard my Team say to me, *"When you shift the energy in the higher realms, it shifts the energy in all the realms where you express yourself. Your physical life is the reflection of the higher realms."*

I thought about this concept as I finished my run and swung by the Coffee Cowboy in town to grab a two-shot latte. As I stood in line, a man I had always found attractive approached me and asked if he could buy me my morning coffee. Without my jaw dropping to the ground and without stumbling all over my words, I said, "Sure. That's so kind of you. Thank you." At the end of our casual conversation he said, "You know, you have the most beautiful eyes I've ever seen."

I almost broke down in tears but held it together long enough to say, "Thank you," and hightailed it home for a cold shower. My heart was racing, not from the run or my two shots of espresso, but from his recognition of a deep inner shift that had happened the night before.

Could I hold this energy? Would I succeed in finding a beloved lifelong partner? Was I no longer destined to be alone, wandering the world as a spiritual, untouchable, highly sensitive woman? Time would tell…

Though I was not sure when my beloved would appear, I did know that when you enlist your Higher Self to do the work for you, in the dimension where your blueprints are held, good things can happen remarkably fast.

You can invite your Higher Self to infuse particular vibrations into your blueprints for different aspects of your life. You can ask for greater vibrations of support and flow to be held in your resource/money blueprint. You can ask your Higher Self to infuse vibrations of love and connection into your relationship blueprints. Those vibrations will then reflect into those aspects of your life. The more you acknowledge that your Higher Self is doing the work, the faster the shift will happen.

For when you are working with your blueprints in the higher realms, you are using your Higher Self, not your mind. I have mentioned this before, but it bears repeating, since it is a key component of the work. You can use your mind to make the request, and then let the wiser, higher, energetic aspect of you do the work. Once the request is made, let it go. Your Higher Self will do the work for you. The shift will be gentle and balanced. It may feel like a release inside you, a swirl of energy like an invisible wind. It can be a flash of light, a deep breath, or a wave of relief. Your body might twitch as the energy moves. You might feel surges and sensations happening in different parts of your body. It is however you perceive it, no matter how subtle. If it is not subtle and seems uncomfortable, ask your Higher Self to slow down and turn down the energetic volume.

Slowly, bit by bit, the energy in these other dimensions will become easier to sense. You will become more aware of the higher energetic aspect of you (your Higher Self). You will develop your energetic senses. What seems unreal will become real. You will be living a conscious, multidimensional reality. Anyone can do this.

It's just a matter of paying attention to what is going on around you and within you, and using the other dimensions as a resource.

I encourage you to be an honest skeptic. Test out the protocols and meditations at the end of this chapter. Notice if you sense an inner shift. If you do, give your Higher Self the credit.

The Physical Dimension as Mirror

If you want to shift the energy in the physical dimension, you need to first shift it in the higher realms. Before we talk more about that, let's take a moment to explore more deeply the nature and factors that create the physical dimension. I think of the physical realm as the surface of a mirror. All the energy held in the higher dimensions is reflected in the physical plane.

This insight occurred one afternoon while I was hiking in the Sierra Nevada foothills. I took a trail I had never been on before. After a few miles, I came upon a little lake nestled at the end of a meadow. I walked to a lone tree at the edge of the water. A flat granite rock next to the tree created the perfect seat. As I sat on the warm rock at the water's edge, the wind began to die down. After a time, I could see the reflection of the tree on the water. As I admired this upside-down image, I felt my angelic guides gathering around me in the higher realms. Little swirls of energy wafted down to me, and I felt dizzy. I brought my energy deep inside my divine line and quieted my mind so that I could hear their wisdom.

Sitting there, watching, being still, I slowly realized, with the help of my guides, that the physical world is a reflection. The combination of the multiple dimensions is what creates this reflection. As I looked at the tree being reflected on the water, I thought about the energetic aspect of me that is my Higher Self.

I saw that the tree and the clouds in the sky were symbolic of my Higher Self and the energy in the higher realms. It was all reflected onto the surface of the water. I realized that if I wished to change the reflection on the water, I had to change the tree or the energy around the tree. I learned not to go to the reflection to make the change, but to my Higher Self. If I adjusted the energy there, it would be reflected in my physical world. The stiller I was inside myself, the less wind there would be on the water. The reflection would have less distortion. The light in my divine line and my Higher Self wisdom would be revealed more clearly in my physical world.

I sat until the wind picked up and the reflection of the tree vanished. As I digested this new insight, I realized that if I was only aware of the reflection on the water, whenever the wind blew I would be lost. If I held my awareness at the level of my Higher Self and in my divine line, when the wind blew (drama happened), I would not lose track of my true self.

In that moment, I fully grasped the concept that if I really wanted to change my life, I had to go to my Higher Self to shift the energy in the higher dimensions first.

Another way to think of the physical dimension is to think of it as the bottom of the ocean. Whatever you drop into the water at the surface eventually ends up on the ocean floor. Imagine your Higher Self lounging on the deck of your luxury yacht. Your Higher Self tosses a bundle of self-love overboard. This love bundle floats down to you as you sit on the ocean floor. When it arrives you feel a swelling of self-love. It is that simple. Really! The less you try with your mind, and the more you enlist your Higher Self to activate particular vibrations and reflect that energy to you, the fuller your life will become.

Insights and Things to Remember

- Being in the physical dimension allows you to shift the vibrations in the higher realms, which in turn reflect into the physical plane.

- When you wish to change the energy in the physical realm, ask for the energy in the higher realms to shift.
- I recommend focusing on shifting *qualities*, not specific outcomes. When the quality shifts, the outcomes will follow naturally and easily. I will discuss this more in chapter 3.
- Any time you shift your awareness from the physical dimension into another dimension, get in and stay in your divine line (elevator shaft) as you travel up or down into other dimensions. Firmly attach your divine line to the front of your spine. Strap in before you drive. The journey is much safer this way.
- Any time you feel an inner shift as a result of the work, ask that all your reference points be updated. Imagine going to the gas station and filling up with fuel, then tapping your fuel gauge to update your new fuel level.

THE HOW

For many years I was a seminar-attending, information-gathering, book-reading spiritual junkie. For all that investment of time and money, I found very few teachers who told me exactly how to do the work. I was told to move into my heart, to feel compassion, and to be nonjudgmental, but not *how* to do it. I found this common problem of spiritual teaching to be very frustrating. So at the end of every chapter, I am going to explain the "how" of the "what." I will give you specific instructions to help your Higher Self do the work.

All the tools and wisdom I am sharing are based on my own experience and that of my clients. Although none of my perspectives are scientifically based, they have proved to be experientially true. You must test the concepts and protocols against your own experience to see if it is *your* cup of tea.

Below you will find a quick protocol, as well as an in-depth one, to help you connect with your divine line and firmly attach it to the front of your spine. You will also find both types of protocols for shifting your blueprints. Follow the steps, and let yourself feel the shift. For all the full protocols in the chapters, you can speak the steps that are in italics either out loud or silently. Some people feel that saying something out loud creates a greater impact and resonance. I believe both ways work. Do what feels appropriate.

In the beginning, I recommend doing the full protocol. Once you have practiced it a few times, your energy fields will get stronger and will automatically bring your awareness into your divine line without your making the full request.

The Quick Steps

Using your imagination, intent, and breath, bring your awareness into your divine line. Firmly attach your divine line to the front of your spine. Hold your awareness in your divine line, and explore the vibration and the light that flows in your divine line. Travel up your divine line to the level of your Higher Self. Explore this expanded higher vibrational aspect of you. When it feels appropriate, travel back down your divine line. Hold your awareness on the front of your spine. Update your reference points.

The Full Protocol

1. *"I invite my Higher Self to work with my energetic fields and the guides to bring all energetic orientation points and awareness off of everything and everyone and back to my*

divine line, which flows on the front of my spine." (Your energetic orientation points are what you use to energetically locate energetic aspects of yourself, resources, and information.)

2. Use your conscious breath. On a deep inhale, imagine pulling yourself into your inner river of light, which flows up and down the front of your spine.

3. Close your eyes, and imagine standing in a column of light. Let the column be as wide as feels comfortable. The more you hold your awareness in your divine line, the wider it will become. (If this is uncomfortable, open your eyes and take a few deep breaths. Focus on something else. Bring your awareness to your feet and then to the top of your head. Tap on your sternum [breastbone], and make low grunting sounds. If that does not alleviate the discomfort, take a shower, go for a walk, eat something, or listen to your favorite music. Go slowly when you are connecting with that divine aspect of you for the first time. Before you can even get in your divine line, you might need to just hold awareness that you actually do have a beautiful river of light flowing on the front of your spine. Do this for a few weeks before you do this protocol again.)

4. Once your awareness or imagination is in your divine line, make the following request: *"I invite my Higher Self to use my energetic fields to firmly attach my divine line to the front of my spine."*

5. Imagine some energetic aspect of you gently yet firmly attaching your divine line all the way up and down the front of your spine. Check your lower spine (your lumbar, waist region). That is the place where you really want

to be firmly attached to the front of your spine. Think of it as the place where you "buckle up."

6. Take a few minutes, and hold your awareness in your divine line. Imagine a beautiful current of energy and light flowing vertically inside you. You may experience the energy flowing up and/or down. It does go both ways. Keep your eyes closed, and explore the layers and vibrations that are held in this inner river of light. Remember, this light is your essence and is perfect and whole. You are a beautiful beam of light.

7. While holding your awareness in your divine line and firmly attaching to the front of your spine, imagine traveling up your divine line to your Higher Self. Stay in your elevator shaft, and push the button for your Higher Self floor. Imagine traveling up and the elevator doors opening at the level of your Higher Self. Stay in your elevator, and perceive reality from the dimension of your energetic self. It will feel lighter and more expanded.

8. *"I ask my Higher Self to work with my energetic fields to activate the vibration of connection, self-love, and peace at the level of my Higher Self and in my divine line."*

9. Imagine your Higher Self doing this work, and when your time on your Higher Self floor feels complete, travel back down your divine line to the front of your spine. Snuggle up on the front of your spine with your inhale, imagination, and intent.

10. Update all your reference points and all your ways of perceiving and being perceived: *"I ask my Higher Self to update all my reference points and all my ways of perceiving and being perceived."*

Explore the sensation of holding more of your awareness in this inner river. Do you feel calmer? Stronger? Happier? Tired?

Whatever the sensation, give yourself a moment to adjust to this different, more connected way of being.

If you do not feel any different, be patient. Every day take one conscious breath, and imagine pulling yourself into your own beautiful inner river of light. You can write this on a little yellow sticky note: "Using my inhale I pull myself into my divine line where I am safe, perfect, connected, and calm." Every time you see this sticky note, your energy fields will automatically trigger a breath, and some part of you will begin to hold more of your awareness in your divine line. This is a little sip from the Seventh Cup.

When you travel up to your Higher Self, you can make requests and get energetic information from your body deva, Team, and guides. We will explore that process in the chapters to come.

You can also use the online audio meditation to help you increase your connection to your divine line and Higher Self.

SHIFTING YOUR BLUEPRINTS

Once you are in your divine line, attached to the front of your spine, and connected to your Higher Self, you can shift your blueprints.

As mentioned earlier, you have specific blueprints for each area of your life. If you shift your resource blueprint in the higher realm, you will eventually experience a physical change in your financial reality. The same is true for your love life, creative expression, and health.

THE QUICK STEPS

Think of which aspect of your life you would like to shift: relationships, resources, creative expression, or health. Bring your awareness into your divine line. Hold your awareness there, and send the request to your Higher Self. You can even imagine sending an email to your Higher Self with your request. You can also travel up your divine line to your Higher Self and make the request. Invite your Higher Self to work with your energetic fields and the guides to locate this particular blueprint. Ask to activate and infuse these intended vibrations in your divine line and into that blueprint. Hold the awareness that your Higher Self is doing this work. Once you feel the shift, update all your reference points and all the ways in which you perceive and are perceived. You are done. Let the work reflect from the higher realms to you in this physical realm.

For a deeper shift, use the following full protocol to shift the blueprint you intend. You can speak the steps in italics out loud or silently.

THE FULL PROTOCOL

1. Get clear about the aspect of your life you would like to shift: the blueprint for your relationships; your resource blueprint, which holds the energy for your money, your health, or any resource that supports you; or your creativity blueprint, which holds your passion, mastery, purpose, service, and right livelihood.

2. Think of the qualities you would like this aspect of your life to hold. Some examples are greater connection, support, abundance, joy, love, empowerment, flow, ease, compassion, and kindness.

3. Take a deep, conscious breath. Imagine pulling yourself into your divine line. Say the request silently or out loud: *"I invite my Higher Self to work with my energetic fields*

    and the guides to pull all my awareness and reference points into my divine line."

4.   *"I invite my Higher Self to work with my energetic fields and the guides to locate my _____ blueprint."*

5.   *"I invite my Higher Self to activate and infuse the vibrations of _____ in my divine line and into my _____ blueprint."*

6.   Hold the awareness that your Higher Self is doing the work in the higher realms. Imagine or sense these qualities flowing in your divine line and being infused into this energetic blueprint. Imagine it reflecting down to you in the physical realm.

7.   *"I invite my Higher Self to update all my reference points and all the ways in which I perceive and am perceived in all realms."*

First Cup Audio Meditations

To listen to the audio meditations for the First Cup, go to www.cupsofconsciousness.com/meditations.

Connecting to Your Divine Line

This meditation is an energetic protocol to help you bring all your reference points for connection back to your divine line. Use your breath to pull yourself into your inner river of light. Firmly attach your divine line to the front of your spine. Activate the vibration of your essence as you hold your awareness in your divine line.

Connecting with Your Higher Self

This meditation supports your energetic fields in connecting with your Higher Self. Use it to activate a greater connection to that wiser, powerful aspect of you and to open the lines of communication between you and your Higher Self.

Activating Your Blueprints

Energetically locate the specific aspect of your life, or blueprint, you wish to shift. Infuse this blueprint with the vibrations, sounds, shapes, and qualities that hold the template for this specific aspect of your life. Activate those same vibrations at the level of your Higher Self and inside your divine line. Reflect those vibrations into this blueprint. Invite your body deva and Team to do the same.

Taking Connected Conscious Breaths

This meditation will help you use your breath to increase your connection to your divine line and your essence; it walks you through twenty conscious breaths. (Think of it as a little bonus meditation.)

May you gently awaken
to your multidimensional self.

SECOND CUP

You Are Never Alone

> **You are surrounded
> by beings of love and light.**

You may remember that as a child you sensed a presence around you. You might have called this presence by a particular name or just thought of it as your imaginary friend. You may have had several "friends" you talked to during the day. Perhaps they were there for you in the middle of the night if you woke with a fright.

Your friends — your guides and your Team — are all still around you. These beings of love and light can help you. They can support and buffer energy for you. In fact, the primary purpose of your Team is to protect you and to model a connected, balanced, and supportive energy to you. (I capitalize *Team* when referring to this group of energy beings to emphasize their importance in your life.)

As I mentioned before, your Team is similar to your angelic guides, but they never leave you. Your guides, who are beings like archangels or Ascended Masters, come and go, depending on your needs and circumstances.

Your Team is unique to you. Each one of your Team members is here to grow, evolve, and assist you as you journey through life. They are not fragments of you. Rather, they hold their own consciousness, which is similar to your level of consciousness. Your Team may be a little less or a little more evolved than you, but not by much. Think of it like a baseball team. You would not put individuals from a Little League team in with professional players. You are all players on a field holding similar interests, agendas, and levels of mastery.

Your Team has influenced your life since birth. We have all had previous lives and will have future lives in this world or possibly in other realms. If your Team has been with you for several incarnations, you will share experiences and memories.

As your Team members encircle you in another dimension, they influence your state of being and what you create. You will empathically feel the vibrations, emotions, and consciousness they are holding inside themselves. When your Team holds a peaceful energy, you will feel peaceful. If they are anxious, you will feel their anxiety. When you invite your Team to cultivate the inner qualities that support them, you will be positively empathically affected.

When you get acquainted with your Team, you will no longer feel alone on the playing field. Life stops being such a struggle. You can ask your Team to hold energies that assist you instead of limiting you. Using your Team gives you access to amazing resources in different dimensions.

If you are feeling unsupported, your Team might be sleeping

on the job. Like any team members, they need coaching, leadership, direction, and purpose. You are the leader. If you would like greater support in your life, now would be a good time to wake up your Team members and get them to huddle around you.

Use this protocol for a quick Team huddle: *"I ask my Higher Self to connect with my Team Members' Higher Selves, and I ask my Team members at the level of their Higher Selves to encircle me in the higher realms in a way that is loving, supportive, and empowering. I ask that they hold connection, love, and peace in themselves."* Take a moment and imagine your Team encircling you in the higher realms.

After my awakening, I could clearly hear and feel my Team members. They would tell me things that were about to happen. They would advise me on big and small matters, such as what lettuce to buy, what meditation I should do to help release a particular challenge, and whom I should date. I ignored the guidance a few times, and suffered the consequences. After a few calamities, I decided that listening to my Team was in my best interest.

As I explored my relationship with my Team, I pondered the possibility that other people had Teams as well.

The Helping Team Member

Diane came in for an acupuncture session with me two days after a harrowing experience. She had been crossing a street when a huge truck barreled through a stop sign and hit her. Miraculously, she was not killed. She didn't even suffer any broken bones. She did have a lot of bruises and a cervical strain (whiplash), which caused a persistent and debilitating headache.

After three sessions with me, her headache was still not going away. At the time of her fourth session, I was at a loss. She was lying on the table with her eyes closed. I sat down and put my face in my hands and silently asked, "What am I not seeing?"

In response, I saw a being of light standing next to Diane, holding his head. I silently asked him who he was. He responded, "I'm part of her Team. I stepped in front of the truck to absorb the energy of the hit so she would not die."

I was shocked. I had never realized that the energy beings surrounding us could be touched by anything in the physical world. I thought they were impervious to such things.

"Are you open to a healing?" I asked him, and he responded, "Yes." I silently asked for angelic healers to surround him and to bring in healing vibrations to help him release his pain. I sat in stillness and watched the angelic healers work with him. After a few minutes he took his hands down from his head and smiled. "Thank you. I am no longer in pain." I replied with a silent "Wonderful."

Diane opened her eyes and said, "Aleya, my headache is gone!"

Your Team can help you. They are standing right next to you, but in another dimension. Your energy fields will pick up the vibration of your Team's energy fields. You may feel your Team members' feelings. I call this empathic dimensional sensitivity. You are literally feeling the emotions and sensations of another being who exists in a different dimension. Your Team members feel energy just like you. If your Team is happy, you will feel happy. If you are frustrated, your Team may feel your feelings and be frustrated as well.

Working with Your Team

Your Team may appear to you as a group or as individuals. I have seen as many as fifteen members on a Team, and as few as two. Honor however you perceive your Team. Furthermore, your Team members have their own divine lines and divine sparks in the heart of Source. They also have Higher Selves that use their energy fields to shift their energy.

Ask your Team members to increase their connection to their own essence and their own divine lines. Urge your Team members to acknowledge and appreciate themselves to a greater degree. When each member acknowledges his or her own presence, you will have a much stronger sense of your Team.

Spend time talking with your Team. Invite your Team to go on a walk with you. When you go to sleep at night, make a request that you and your Team heal, release, align, and connect in healthier, happier ways.

Invite your Team members to help you. Ask them to gather appropriate information and resources. Invite them to engage in specific behaviors will that support you in your daily life. When it is tax time, I ask at least one of my Team members to put on an accounting hat so that I can engage in the task of number crunching with joy and confidence instead of dread.

When I was studying for my pilot's license in 2006, I sent my Team off to master takeoffs and landings. The next day, I found that my piloting skills had improved dramatically. My flight instructor had no idea what had happened. She just attributed it to something inside me "clicking." I have to give the credit to my Team. They held a certain level of mastery regarding flight. They modeled that to me, and I was empathically affected.

The following protocol will help you connect with your Team members.

CONNECTING WITH YOUR TEAM

Take a breath. Pull all your awareness into your divine line. Firmly attach your divine line to the front of your spine. Set the intention, and imagine traveling up to your Higher Self. (Take your glass elevator up to your Higher Self floor.) Ask your Higher Self to connect with the Higher Selves of your Team. The specific words for this request follow:

1. *"I invite my Higher Self to work with my energetic fields and the guides to connect with the Higher Selves of my Team members."* Invite them to huddle around you. Imagine them either as a group or as individuals. However you imagine them is fine. There is no right or wrong way.
2. *"I ask that my Team, which is of love and light, surround me at the level of my Higher Self."*
3. *"I ask that each member of my Team, at the level of their Higher Selves, work with their energetic fields and the guides to connect with their own divine lines and remember their own essence."*
4. *"I invite my Team members to remember their agreement to support, buffer, and model a positive energy to me as I journey in this world."*
5. *"I invite my Team members at the level of their Higher Selves to work with their energetic fields and the guides to hold love, gentleness, and support in their own divine lines."*

Take a breath, and hold awareness that some part of you and your Team knows how to do this. After each request, take a moment and let the work happen in a higher realm. The protocols are not something you want to speed-read. Let yourself move into a slow dreamy state while reading or speaking them.

You can imagine watching your Higher Self connecting with your Team. Try not to use the mind to do the work; let your Higher Self do it. Use your imagination to *see* it happening. You can ask and imagine your Higher Self blowing the "gather the Team" whistle when you want your Team to huddle around you.

You may feel a slight shift in the energy around you after you make this request. A huge swell of emotions, tears, or relief may wash over you. If that happens — and I hope you are not riding on a crowded subway when it does! — simply let the emotions move through you.

If you don't feel anything, don't worry; nothing is wrong. Be patient with the process, since it might take a while before you perceive your Team. Every morning when you wake up, or every evening when you go to bed, simply acknowledge the presence of your Team. Say, "Good morning, Team," or "Good night, Team." After a few weeks of greeting them and saying good night to them, come back to the protocol for connecting with your Team, and try it again. See if the process feels different. You can also listen to the audio meditation for connecting with your Team at the end of this chapter.

EMPATHIC SENSITIVITY AND YOUR TEAM

Your Team greatly influences the way you feel and the way you respond to the physical world. Again, when you help your Team members shift how they feel inside, you will be positively affected.

As I continued to work with people's Teams, I learned more and more about how our Teams affect us. I had a particularly interesting experience with one of my clients. Annie came in for an energy-balancing session after six weeks of unusual depression. As she sat down, she said, "I know this sounds really extreme, and I haven't told anyone how I am really feeling. But six weeks ago I started feeling really depressed. I feel like I'm done. Like I should just leave."

"Do you mean leave Telluride or leave the planet?"

With tears welling up in her eyes she said, "Leave the planet. I feel like I have done everything I came here to do and that perhaps my time in this world is coming to an end. It's weird. I do not feel suicidal; I just feel done."

I invited her to climb up on the table, and I scanned her energy fields, looking for the root of the challenge. A few moments later, one of her Team members came forward. He was very pushy, and he said to me, "It's my turn now. I am the one who should be in the physical realm, not her. Her turn is over."

"Oh, really? And why is that?" I silently asked.

"I can do life in the physical dimension much better than she can. I know so much more, and I would be able to live a better and more productive life."

I responded, "Would you be willing to first share all this information with Annie's Higher Self?"

He briefly hesitated, nodded his head, and then started sending his wisdom.

Annie said, "Aleya, I don't know what's happening, but when I close my eyes all I can see is light, and I'm feeling lighter and lighter. What's going on?"

I said, "I was just having a silent conversation with one of your Team members. This particular Team member was very pushy."

Before I got a chance to continue, she said, "Oh, my God, I can't believe you're saying this. For the past two weeks I have felt literally pushed, like someone was pushing me out of my life. Does that make sense?"

I responded, "Yes, it does. This Team member thought that he could somehow do it better and that it should be his turn. He said it was because he felt like he had lots of information and ways of doing things that might be better than yours. I asked him if he would be willing to share this information with you at the level of your Higher Self. When he started to send the information, you started seeing light, and I started to feel an expansion and a lightening happen in your energetic fields."

I asked Annie if we could keep going, since I wanted to see if there were any other layers, and I also wanted to hold space for a greater exchange of information between Annie and this Team member. "Annie, I invite you to use your imagination, and even more important, to ask your Higher Self, to locate and connect with the Team member who has this information for you."

She said, "I feel a very pushy energy. I feel like he is telling me I am not doing something right."

I invited her to probe more deeply and connect with this Team member. "Can you imagine a being standing near you?"

"Yes, I actually see him, if my eyes are closed."

"Say hi, and let him know you see him," I instructed.

"I see you," Annie said out loud.

As soon as she spoke those words, she started crying. "I can see him, and he just started to cry. He said that he has wanted so much to help me, but I never listened, and he didn't think I even knew he existed. He feels acknowledged for the first time."

As tears ran down her face, I asked my guides what to do next.

"Have her Team member connect and recognize his own essence. Have him open the lines of communication with her and hold patience in himself as he models right energy to Annie."

I spoke these instructions to her Team member and said, "Annie, ask your Team member to recognize himself more deeply and feel his divine line, which carries his essence." Before these words were even out of my mouth, the room filled with a thick mist of white light.

Annie said, "He took a look within and saw a thin line of light, and as soon as he recognized that it was his energy, he got enveloped in his own white light. I can still see him, but he looks much lighter and happier."

I asked her Team member, "Are you comfortable standing in

another dimension and continuing to hold vigil and relay information, instead of kicking her out so you can be next?"

I could feel him step back and hold a sweet supportive energy. He said, "Yes. I will hold patience and compassion and model right energy to her."

Annie breathed a breath of relief and smiled, and her body relaxed for the first time in six weeks.

When her Team member shifted, Annie felt a level of confidence and support she had been yearning for. When you help your Team members shift and hold qualities that are supportive, you too will experience wonderful changes in your life. It is easy and faster for your Team members to shift the energy inside themselves, since they do not have to deal with the density of the physical realm.

The important thing to remember when you work with your Team members is to invite them to shift their own vibrations, as opposed to doing it for them. Let them do their own inner work. The more you let them be responsible for themselves, the stronger your Team members will become. One way to help your Team is to model to them the energy you want them to embody in your own self. If you want your Team to be calm and confident, ask your Higher Self to activate those vibrations at the level of your Higher Self and in your divine line. Imagine a calm, confident stream of energy flowing in your divine line. Stand in that current, and model this energy to your Team. Invite them to activate their own inner currents of calm confidence in their own divine lines.

In my own life, I slowly learned how to be in a healthy co-creative relationship with my Team instead of a codependent one. The first step is to be responsible for your own energy and no one else's. This process is slow, but over time, it yields huge results.

Your Team wants to help you. Invite each of your Team members to help you by modeling right energy to you. Remind them to be more responsible for their own energy than for yours.

Holding Attachment Appropriately

All of us have felt burned out at one time or another. I know I have.

Imagine working sixteen-hour days for several years and never taking a weekend off, much less a vacation. Imagine thinking that you are a slacker, no matter how hard you work. Eventually the burn-out button will get pushed. I engaged in this experiment a few years back. Insanity? Yes, but it was a worthwhile experience.

After a year of workaholism, I began to wonder why I had fallen into such unbalanced behavior. I sent the question up to my Higher Self. After several days of scanning the higher realms, checking my Soul and body, and asking myself whether this might be empathic sensitivity coming from a client, I heard the word *Team.*

I was standing at the kitchen sink, washing the dinner dishes at the end of another long day. I turned the water off for a moment and dropped deep inside my divine line. As I brought my awareness there, I silently invited my Team to huddle around me. I traveled up my divine line to the level of my Higher Self and invited my Higher Self to connect with the Higher Selves of my Team members. Holding my awareness in this higher realm as I scrubbed the frying pan, I silently said, "So, what gives with you guys? Who's the workaholic?" I felt one of my Team members sheepishly come forward.

Acknowledging his presence I asked, "Why are you holding this workaholic behavior?"

My Team member responded, "Well, do you remember when you wanted help getting rid of your habit of procrastination about a year ago? I thought that if I held the workaholic vibe, that might help you break through the procrastinator energy. In truth, I am totally exhausted at a Soul level, and I think I might need a vacation."

I laughed out loud and asked, "Would you be up for holding a different vibration to help me with my procrastination?"

My Team member responded, "I think if I hold the vibration of focus and discipline, it will help you and will not work us all into the ground."

"Brilliant!" I said. "Would you be up for shifting the energy inside yourself and then taking a respite in whatever dimension you choose?"

When he happily agreed, I silently said, "I invite my Team member at the level of his Higher Self to work with his energetic fields and the guides to release all workaholic behaviors for helping me release procrastination. I invite him to lift all his attachment and his desire for me to be productive, focused, and disciplined off of me and put it back onto himself.

"Only when you are attached to your own energy and behavior will you be able to create a strong coherent field of transformation and positively impact another."

I continued, "I invite my Team member to hold responsibility for his own inner focus, discipline, and drive. I ask that he activate the vibration of focus, discipline, and drive in his own divine line as he stands next to me in another dimension."

I took a deep breath and wiped my hands on the dishcloth. I leaned up against the counter and waited. I could feel little swirls of energy around me, and the heavy veil of workaholism began to lift. For the first time in months, I felt light in my heart.

My sweet dog, Freckles, got off the couch and came into the kitchen, wagging his tail. He must have felt the shift around me as well. I gleefully threw on my jacket and took him for a long walk under the stars.

As I walked and felt the expansiveness within and around me, I checked in with my Team members, specifically the one who had just shifted so dramatically. "How are you doing?" I silently asked.

Instead of hearing words, I felt a huge rush of love hit my heart. I burst into tears and laughter at the same time and silently said with a smile, "That good, huh?"

After this shift in my Team member, I felt a new rhythm. I gave myself permission to play, and I felt a fresh desire to dive into projects. I was surprised at how motivated I was after giving myself a little guiltless break and letting one of my Team members get some much-needed rest.

My Team member had been trying to help, but he was using an unhealthy behavior to address the need. That is often the case; although a behavior addresses a need, it may be inefficient.

When I invited my Team member to let go of his attachment to my process and to model a healthier solution, my workaholic behavior completely shifted. I know that my Team member just wanted to help me and was doing so the best way he knew how. But there is usually a better way.

When you can no longer tolerate an unhealthy behavior, it is an indicator that you are ready to hunt down the root and release the unhealthy pattern. You are ready for a change.

When you have an issue you would like to shift, check to see if one of your Team members is holding that behavior inside. Invite him or her to release it and to bring in a healthier behavior to replace it.

I realized, after trial and error, that I could only shift the issues and energies that were mine. If my Team members had issues that I thought were mine, the energy would not shift. If I handed the responsibility for shifting the issue back to my Team members and held space for them to shift it, the issue would resolve. If the issue did not belong to them, I would invite them to send it, and any information they might have regarding the issue, to whomever owned the issue. The challenge would then promptly release.

Here are a few tips for building a sustainable relationship with your Team members.

- Let your Team members use their energy to shift themselves. Do not use your energy to shift them.
- Invite your Team members to return all the responsibility they are holding that belongs to you.
- Return all responsibility for your Team members that you might be holding for them.
- Invite your Team members to be attached to, desire, and be responsible for only the energy they hold inside themselves, not the energy of one another, you, your body deva, or anyone else.
- Invite your Team members to hold the qualities, emotions, and behaviors they want you to embody in themselves, and to model that to you.
- Your Team members can only shift their own issues and no one else's.

WHAT IF THERE'S NO TEAM?

Your Team can be one of your greatest resources for support. If your Team members are sleeping on the job, you will feel alone and unsupported. Every client I have worked with in the past decade has had a Team, except one…

Mike was in his midthirties, working odd jobs in Telluride. He was often out of work and struggled to make ends meet, and his relationships with women never seemed to last. Mike came in for a session one day with his head hung low. I wondered if he was between women or jobs or just had his usual hangover.

"Aleya, it just seems like everything is a struggle. Nothing is easy, and I feel totally alone. I have great friends, I love where I live, but I feel empty inside. I feel like no one really understands me. Hell, I don't feel like I understand myself. It's as if there's no one in my life supporting me. I feel so lost, and I'm really confused."

I could hear and feel his frustration and confusion. I put a few acupuncture needles in him to help alleviate his anxiety. "Mind if I do some energy work with you?" I asked.

When he agreed, I placed my hands on his feet, and dropping into a very still space, I thought to myself, "Maybe I should check on his Team."

I brought my awareness up into a higher realm and viewed Mike through my Higher Self lens.

I asked his Team to appear. As soon as I made the request, I started to feel an empty energy that was really uncomfortable. I began to panic as the emptiness settled in, but I continued, searching for any sign of his Team. I couldn't see or feel anything.

A few months earlier, I had started working with a guide in the higher realms during my healing sessions. He would answer my questions and kept me pointed in the right direction. As I felt another huge wave of anxiety and confusion, I called in my guide and asked, "What's happening? What does this mean?"

My guide answered, "He chose not to have a Team. He came into this world determined to prove to himself that he can do it alone."

That explained the problem. Without a Team, everything in life would be a struggle. No wonder Mike felt so isolated and alone.

"What do I do?" I silently asked.

"First, connect with Mike's Higher Self at the level of your Higher Self."

My guide continued to instruct me. He said, "Now ask Mike's Higher Self where his Team is."

When I asked, his Higher Self responded, "I decided to incarnate without one. I thought I could go it alone."

"Would you like to have an angelic support Team at this time?" I asked.

At the level of his Higher Self, I could see Mike struggling with this question. As he paused, I thought about his needing to prove his strength. Another question arose inside me. "What if he accessed the vibration of strength inside himself instead of having to prove his strength by going it alone?"

I invited Mike's Higher Self to locate his strength deep in his core. Holding my awareness at the level of my Higher Self, I demonstrated the energy I was inviting him to embrace. I brought my awareness to my own divine line. I invited my Higher Self to activate the vibration of strength in my divine line. As I felt this current of strength inside me, I invited Mike's Higher Self to do the same.

I could see Mike's Higher Self connecting with and gathering his own little balls of light, which held the vibration of strength. It was almost funny, as if he were using a cosmic vacuum cleaner to suck all those "strength balls" back into himself.

Mike said, "Wow, what's happening, Aleya? I am seeing this huge waterfall of white light, and I feel like I am getting filled up with it. I kind of feel like I'm tripping. What's going on?"

I began, "So, Mike, you know how I am working with the energy fields more and more these days? Well, the more I work with it, the more I am learning. In this moment I saw your Higher Self. It is the energetic aspect of you that hangs out in a higher dimension.

"I am also aware of and work with an energy that is called a Team. It is an energy consciousness that surrounds you in another dimension. Kids sometimes see their Teams as imaginary friends."

He frowned and said, "I didn't have any imaginary friends as a kid."

"Umm, I know. It feels to me as if you don't have a Team around you at all. I was just having a conversation with your Higher Self to see if you would be up for bringing in a Team. To be honest, I am still new to all this, and I might be wrong. But we could do a little work and see if you feel better."

He started to tear up. "This is weird. I am feeling all this sadness. If what you say is right, it makes perfect sense. I have always felt like I have had to prove I can do it by myself. I am so tired. I don't want to do it alone anymore."

"Well, if you really did want to do it alone, you would have decided to incarnate on a planet where you were the only being. Instead, you chose to incarnate in a world that has billions of people and zillions of angels. So, this is not the best place to go it alone," I laughed.

"Yeah, you're telling me. Do your mojo, Aleya. I'm ready for a change."

I nodded and waited for his energy fields to balance and align.

"Mike, I am going to talk with your Higher Self and have a conversation about bringing in a Team that can support you. Do you want me to do this out loud or silently?"

Mike asked me to do it out loud, so I said, "Higher Self of Mike, how do you feel about having a Team that can support you in this world?"

I could see Mike's Higher Self looking around him and then agreeing. "I invite you, Mike, at the level of your Higher Self, to work with your energetic fields, your angelic advisers, and your guides and to connect with a Team of beings of love and light who can support you. Let your Team be of a similar vibration and consciousness and have similar lessons to learn. Let your Team members buffer and protect you, hold appropriate boundaries around themselves, and model a balanced and connected energy to you."

Within a few minutes, we could both feel his new Team gathering around him. The whole room started to fill with light. As his new Team came into place, I could hear laughter coming from the higher realms.

Mike started to laugh. I quickly pulled the needles out of his arms and feet. After a few minutes, the energy around him settled, and I felt a deep sense of gratitude and calm.

I quietly said, "Team, huddle up around Mike, buffer him, model right energy to him, and hold your wisdom in yourself. Thank you for holding space for him as he journeys in this life."

Mike smiled and said, "I can see them. I can hear them. This is super cool and kind of weird." Tears of relief continued to flow. His Team huddled around him and gently showered Mike with love. As Mike got off the table, he reported sensing greater support and connection. He said he felt as if he now had more resources to assist him in his journey.

I continued to see Mike for the next three years. In that time, he accomplished more than he ever had before. Struggles still arose, but now he had tools and support. There was a sense of joy in his heart. He was no longer alone. A year after the session described above, his physical life started to reflect his energetic life. He got engaged to a great woman and started a thriving business.

As I said, Mike's lack of a Team was unique. I have worked with thousands of people, and he is the only person I have met who did not have a Team. In general, I find that though the majority of people do have Teams, they have not consciously connected with them. The more aware you are of your Team, the more present, supportive, and powerful they will become.

After Mike's session, I started checking in with my own Team members. I spent hundreds of hours talking to them and learning how to work with them in a healthy way. I asked my Team members to start holding particular vibrations and behaviors inside themselves as they surrounded me. If I felt anxious, I would ask them to hold a vibration of calm. As soon as my Team members shifted their own energy, my energy would shift, usually within a few minutes.

If your Team loses its inspiration or passion, you will feel it. You may interpret the loss as your own, instead of realizing that it is a Team issue.

Your Team members may have agendas and desires that could affect you. If you are aware of those agendas, you can change them. When the Team's agenda aligns with your agenda, your reality changes in a delightful way.

Your Team members need to hold appropriate boundaries for themselves. They are responsible for modeling a coherent energy field to you. You may need to remind them about this responsibility from time to time.

If you yearn for a greater connection with your Team members, remember to connect with yourself. When you try to connect with your Team members and you are not holding your awareness in your divine line, you may not feel a strong connection with them.

There is no perfect way or right way to talk to your guides and Team. Just start connecting with them in your own unique way.

CLEAN UP YOUR TEAM

If you find that your Team is not shifting, make sure that everyone on your Team truly belongs. Make sure there are no hitchhikers, that is, beings who are not part of your core group. *Members only!*

Invite your Team members at the level of their Higher Selves to see if there is anyone around them in another dimension who is lost or does not belong to the core group. If one of your Team members does find beings who are not part of your core group, invite the guides to help clear off these nonmembers.

Ask that these beings who are lost or who do not belong be taken to their right and perfect place. Ask your Team members to return any Soul fragments or responsibilities that they are holding for any nonmember. (These fragments are little aspects of your light that can be taken by others during trauma or in unhealthy relationships. When you retrieve your Soul fragments, you experience an inner wholeness.) Ask your Team members to relay all relevant and appropriate information from their Higher Selves to the nonmembers' Higher Selves.

Ask your Team members to clear themselves of all energy that does not belong to them. Ask your Team to hold its own energy, issues, and karma and no one else's. It is your Team members' job to hold a clean space and to hold appropriate boundaries around themselves. You can remind them from time to time, but let them do the work.

INSIGHTS AND THINGS TO REMEMBER

- Your Team members surround you in another dimension that is just a finger's breadth away.
- You and your Team hold a similar level of consciousness.
- Each one of your Team members signed up to buffer, support, learn from, and grow with you during this incarnation.
- The energy they hold inside themselves can positively or negatively affect you.
- Since your Team does not have to deal with the density of the physical dimension, it is easier and faster for them to shift their energy than it is for you to shift it your own.
- You and your Team may have had many lives together in many different forms and dimensions.

THE HOW

Let's dive into the spiritual lab and use the quick steps and the full protocol, which will help you connect and communicate more easily with your Team.

Your Higher Self can open lines of communication between you and your Team. Once the connection opens, you will feel your Team around you. As you connect with your Team members, you can help them shift how they feel inside themselves. If you would like to connect with your Team more deeply, you can either listen to the meditation at the end of this chapter or read the following protocols.

THE QUICK STEPS

Connect with your Team members at the level of their Higher Selves. Invite your Team members to bring all their awareness back to their divine lines. Invite them to recognize their position and to buffer, support, and protect themselves and to model that to you. At the level of your Higher Self, set up grids of connection between you and your Team's Higher Selves. Invite your Team members, as they encircle you, to activate the vibrations of connection and empowerment in their divine lines.

A FEW MORE TECHNIQUES FOR CONNECTING WITH YOUR TEAM

Invite your guides and your Team to encircle you in the higher realms. (Create a safe space for yourself.) Invite your Higher Self to energetically open your ears to receiving information from your Team. Take a moment to imagine your Higher Self cleaning, clearing, and recalibrating your energetic eyes, energetic ears, and heart to open to receive your own inner wisdom, as well as the wisdom coming from your Team. Release all distorted listening mechanisms that are affecting your natural ability to receive pure, true information from yourself and your Team. Repair all the ways in which you receive information.

Invite yourself as a future Ascended Master to repair all the listening mechanisms that help you receive information from the angelic beings of love and light. Ask your Higher Self to create and activate the grids for open lines of communication between you and your Team. Invite and allow for an energetic exchange of information between you and your Team at the level of your Higher Selves. Ask for the appropriate shapes, sounds, and vibrations to activate around you in a way that supports you in receiving the appropriate information from your Team.

As you move through your day, imagine your Team members encircling you and holding love inside themselves. Invite them to model an empowered connected energy to you.

Below is the full protocol for connecting with your Team. This will be a more powerful experience than the quick steps. Go slowly, and let yourself feel the shifts. Once again, you can read the parts in italics either silently or out loud.

THE FULL PROTOCOL

1. Take a few deep breaths into your belly (a new technique). As you inhale, imagine bringing your awareness from the future back to this present breath of now. As you exhale, imagine pulling all your energy out of the past and into this present breath of now. Take another few breaths, and pull yourself into your divine line. Hold your awareness

in your divine line, and make this request: *"I invite my Higher Self to work with my energetic fields to bring all my awareness, reference points, and anchors back to my divine line in this present breath of now."*

2. As you hold your awareness in your divine line, imagine your Higher Self above you or around you. You might imagine yourself sitting on a cloud or platform of light, holding great wisdom and a wide perspective. You might imagine your Higher Self having angel wings or as the divine aspect of you that embodies your light body. Your Higher Self exists in a higher dimension that you may perceive above or around you. Either way works.

3. Repeat: *"I ask my Higher Self to connect with the Higher Selves of my Team members."*

4. Take a moment and breathe. Relax your body, and imagine your Higher Self doing this work. Your mind does not need to know how this works. Let go. Allow some other, wiser aspect of you to connect with these beings of love and light. You may feel a slight shift within or around you as your Higher Self makes this connection.

5. Ask your Team members at the level of their Higher Selves to connect with their own essence: *"I invite my Team members at the level of their Higher Selves to connect with their own essence, which flows in their divine lines."*

6. Invite your Team members to return all the responsibilities they are holding for you: *"I invite my Team members to return all responsibilities that are not theirs back to their right and perfect place, along with all relevant and appropriate information."*

7. Invite your Team members to be responsible only for themselves. Ask them to model healthy energy to one another and to you: *"I invite my Team members to retrieve*

and hold all responsibilities for themselves that they have given to me or to others. I invite my Team members to gather all appropriate resources and information that can help them take full responsibility for supporting, protecting, loving, and honoring themselves."

8. Let go, and allow the work to happen. Bit by bit, your Team members will feel lighter, happier, empowered, and more connected. You, in turn, will feel a higher vibration around you.

9. Think about how you want to feel inside, and ask your Team members to hold those vibrations and energy inside themselves. Ask them to model that energy to you as you move through the day, sleep, dream, and play: *"I invite my Team members to think about the qualities they wish to hold inside themselves."* Wait a moment as they get clear regarding their own intentions. You do not have to know what these qualities are; just hold the intention that they be positive and empowering: *"I invite my Team members at the level of their Higher Selves to activate the qualities they intend for themselves at the level of their Higher Selves and in their own divine lines."*

10. Pause, and hold a gentle awareness that your Team members are activating the desired vibrations and qualities inside their own divine lines as they encircle you in a higher realm.

11. Update all your reference points and those of your Team. *"I ask that all the reference points for me and my Team be updated."*

When your Team holds a happier, higher, and more connected energy, your life becomes happier and more connected. Allow yourself to have conversations with your Team. Treat your

Team the way you want to be treated. Your Team is here to journey with, learn from, and evolve alongside you.

Second Cup Audio Meditation

To listen to the audio meditation for the Second Cup, go to www.cupsofconsciousness.com/meditations.

Connecting with Your Team

This meditation is an energetic protocol to help you connect with your Team. Invite your Higher Self to connect with your Team members at the level of their Higher Selves. Create grids of love and light between you and them. Ask for an appropriate relay of information.

May you feel the love, connection, and support
from the beings of love and light who surround you
in another dimension. They are always with you,
even if you are not conscious of their presence.
Enjoy them; they are an enormous asset.

3 THIRD CUP

You Can Change Your Inner World

> **What you connect with inside yourself is what you create in your outer world. As Gandhi said, be the change you want to see in your world.**

Your life may be filled with beautiful or challenging relationships. Your finances may ebb and flow like the ocean tides. Your body may betray or support you. Whatever your outer world may be, you are the one creating your life. What you focus on is what you create.

This is not a new concept. The movie *The Secret*, and many ancient teachings before it, has taught that your internal reality creates your outer world. But here's the real secret: you shift your outer life by shifting your inner energies, using your Higher Self. If you feel deep support flowing inside you, your outer world will begin reflecting to you greater degrees of support. Simply put, and it bears repeating, changing your inner life will change your outer life.

If the message coming from within is that you are not enough, you will eventually create a situation in which you will not have enough in your outer world. Your bank account may reflect this internal feeling of lack. Your health may fail. You may not have supportive relationships. The longer you hold a particular energy, emotion, belief system, or behavior, the more likely it is to be reflected in your outer life.

The good news is that any impoverished part of your life gives you important information that you can act on. You can use your outer life to find out what is going on energetically. With that information, you can change yourself, your body, and your Team.

STEPS TO CHANGING YOUR INNER LIFE

The first step in changing your inner life requires awareness. Every time you take a breath, you have the opportunity to do an inner check-in. How are you feeling inside right now? Calm, anxious, tired, relaxed? Taking even ten seconds to do a check-in cultivates greater awareness.

But here's the catch. If you are not conscious of something, you cannot change it. The more aware you are, the more you can change. At first this might be a little overwhelming. Perhaps you have already cultivated a certain level of inner awareness but are not sure how to shift your challenges and uncomfortable feelings. Either way, holding awareness is step number one.

Think of your emotions, behaviors, and belief systems simply as compass settings. They are indicators you can use to adjust your direction and what you create for yourself. They are clues to your inner energy patterns. Your increased awareness of your emotions and behaviors gives you the opportunity to change your compass heading.

Step number two speaks to the energy of attachment and desire. What are you attached to, and what do you desire? Are you focused on other people's lives more than on your own? For example, do you want other people to be happy, safe, or supported? Do you want them to be honest and act with integrity and respect?

When you hold your focus on others, you are giving away precious energy. When you focus on yourself, you can shift your internal reality and model that to others.

Perhaps this sounds selfish to you. When I first came across this concept, it struck me this way too, so I sat down in meditation and asked the Ascended Masters, "Is it selfish to be attached only to my own internal reality?" They responded: "That is the only way you can truly help another. If you hold all your attachment on yourself and desire only your own internal reality, you have the capacity to use all your energy to shift yourself. As you shift the vibrations inside you into greater states of love, connection, happiness, self-respect, and peace, you are able to model that higher, more coherent way of being to others.

"You no longer need to change or control another person as a way of alleviating your own anxiety. As you pull your attachment/control and desire off others, you will also release energetic responsibility for other people's lives. The people in your life will in turn move into greater states of personal responsibility and inner empowerment. The more personal responsibility an individual holds, the more empowered he or she becomes.

"As you hold attachment and desire just for yourself, you will no longer project onto others what you think they need. Holding attachment and desire for your internal reality is a more loving way of being. It is not selfish at all. You will be of greater service when you hold this stance."

After this meditative conversation, I also realized how holding attachment and desire for another person's reality can affect integrity and boundaries. If I am attached to another person's behavior, I automatically take responsibility for something that is not mine. I have just crossed someone's boundary and stolen. My new stance quickly became, "Hands to myself; no stealing; model right energy."

Give yourself permission to be attached to your own feelings and internal reality and no one else's. As you hold this stance, coupled with greater inner awareness, you can dive into the next layer of the Third Cup. Drum roll, please! Turn up your courage dial, take a deep breath, and get ready to swallow the...*personal responsibility pill.*

When you take responsibility for your internal reality, reactions, and emotions, you move into the seat of power. You no longer blame people for how you feel. You are no longer a victim or a victimizer. Everything that happens is an opportunity for you to grow (that one is a little sip from the Fourth Cup). As you hold responsibility for your internal reality, emotions, and behavior, you gain control of your life. You can alter your course as you choose.

The Third Cup equation:
Inner awareness + inner attachment
+ personal responsibility + choice = change

As you hold all four of these components inside yourself, you will be able to effect major change in your life. Below I've listed the steps to help you embody all the layers of the Third Cup:

1. Increase awareness of your feelings and how they reflect into your outer world.
2. Hold all your attachment and desire on yourself for your own internal reality.

3. Take responsibility for your own feelings.
4. Choose the energy you want to embody, and invite your Higher Self to get on it. (More about this in "The How" section at the end of this chapter.)

As you work through these layers, be gentle with yourself. Every time you notice a less-than-desirable feeling, crank up that courage dial and hold awareness around the emotion. Just acknowledge it. "I am feeling _____." Sit in the energy for a moment, even if it is uncomfortable. Just observe it. Your mere awareness will begin to shift the energy. As you sit in it, observe it as if it were a wave of energy or an energetic gust of wind moving through you. Emotions are indicators. Use them to point yourself in your intended direction.

Invite your Higher Self to retrieve all your attachment and desire for other people's realities and to be attached only to your own internal reality. Hold and use your energy on yourself.

Next comes the personal responsibility moment. Acknowledge that you have created this situation because of some energy you are connecting with internally. Use your free will and choice to change.

The Fourth Cup will take you deeper into the practice of shifting uncomfortable feelings and challenges. For now, practice cultivating awareness, inner attachment, personal responsibility, and making the choice to change.

A WAKE-UP CALL

Unhealthy behavior can be an uncomfortable wake-up call. Have you ever committed to another person more than to yourself? Have you ever wanted someone to commit to you more than *you* were committed to you?

For me, learning about the Third Cup involved a few boxes of tissue and a pinch of heartache. My inner lack of commitment to myself was being painfully revealed in my dating life — and not for the first time.

I was in love. He was tall, dark, and handsome (of course), an ex–football player, a yoga instructor, and a SNAG (sensitive new age guy) named Andrew. After meeting through a mutual friend, we went from being acquaintances to friends, until one day, after teaching a sound healing yoga class with me, Andrew came over with a big smile, opened his arms, and gave me a hug that lasted longer than a "just friend" hug.

I thought, "Could this really be happening? No way! What does he see in me? I am not a 110-pound yoga bunny! That's his type." I was in disbelief, but deep down inside I was hoping it really *was* happening.

"Do you want to go and get some lunch with me?" he asked.

I gulped for air and could only muster a nod and a smile. We grabbed lunch nearby, and he filled me in on all the cool spots and must-do's in Santa Barbara. For seven magical days we frolicked, hiked, beach-walked, and met his friends, and I successfully forgot myself. He became my everything in seven short days. My entire world revolved around his schedule and his needs. Talk about codependence! I had a case of it, big time. My higher awareness and my connection with my guides and Team took a backseat, or maybe I had put them in the trunk.

After this week of bliss, as we were walking on the beach one morning, I told Andrew, "I have to go back to Telluride in a few days to see clients. But I'll be back in ten days." I looked at him and then gazed out on the calm ocean. The birds were soaring, and I saw a pod of dolphins a hundred feet from shore. It was one of those magical moments when time stops spinning and a sweet blanket of love covers everything. The past week had felt like a delicious eternity to me. Surely he felt the magic too?

He very casually said, "Sure thing. Have a great time."

He did not drop to his knees and plead for me to stay or ask to come with me. Doubt began to creep into my heart. This was not the first time I had hooked up with a guy and lost myself. But usually I got at least three weeks of unhealthy behavior in lustful love before the veil of illusion got yanked away.

"Not so soon," I silently whined to my Team.

I had not yet swallowed the pill of personal responsibility and learned that what you hold inside you is what is reflected back. This lesson had been presented to me twice in the past two years. Andrew was number three. Usually the third time is when the lesson clicks, and I (hopefully) get it. If not, the fourth time is more obvious, requiring even more boxes of tissue.

As I drove out of town, with a fourteen-hour commute in front of me, I fantasized about my future with Andrew. Every time I heard the angelic whispers, I pushed the higher realms' guidance aside.

"What do they know? They aren't here in the flesh. They don't know how it feels," I mumbled to myself.

After fourteen hours of fantasy and delusion, I dove into work. After ten days of seeing clients I jumped back into my car and scurried back to my new life in Santa Barbara. As the long commute began, I thought about my new love. The only problem was that my new love had not called me. I had left him a few messages, with no return call. I thought to myself, "I'm sure he's just really busy."

As I drove across the desert, I was hit by a huge wave of anxiety. After an hour of fretting, I realized that I could not endure any more internal torture. I took a deep breath and brought my awareness into my heart and into my divine line. I imagined opening my energetic ears to my Higher Self. I invited my Higher Self to connect with my guides and Team. As soon as I opened to this shift, a gentle, calm energy washed over me.

I felt into my heart and asked my Higher Self, "Why am I feeling all this anxiety?" I could feel my guides and Team encircling me, holding love and compassion. I could see my Higher Self looking at my infatuation with Andrew from the perspective of an eagle soaring on the updrafts high above its terrain.

After an hour of driving in silence, letting my Higher Self soar and observe, I was finally able to hear my guides. In those days, my guides would give me a pearl once I had completely exhausted myself with emotion, fear, and worry. I suppose it was in those moments when I was most ready for the information. My guides came forth and spoke in a gentle whisper, "This relationship that never was will never be. You must be fully committed to your essence before another can commit to you."

When the guides talk, it's not like a chorus of voices. It's more like thoughts and impressions forming inside my head that I can tell are not mine. There is a different tone, usually more mature, than that of my own thoughts. They communicate by downloading energy, emotions, images, colors, sounds, and sometimes words, all within a few seconds. It is an etheric collage that makes instant sense at an energetic level. But my mind needs time to process all the layers. Processing the energetic information can take a few minutes, hours, or days, depending on the depth of the information relayed. That may be why the guides only give a pearl and then become silent and hold the space for processing.

Lost in the Land of Andrew

The silent desert stretched before me. "Commit to my essence? What does that mean, and what does that really feel and look like?"

I invited my Higher Self to work with my energetic fields and the guides to pull all my commitments off of everyone and everything and bring them back to my divine line. I heard the guides say, "Especially Andrew," so I invited my Higher Self to pull all my commitment, attachment, and desire off of Andrew and back to my own divine line.

I took a breath and released my death grip on the steering wheel. My shoulders relaxed, and I felt a warm rush of energy, coupled with goose bumps, all over my body. Tears started to well up from deep within. Soon I was sobbing, so I pulled over to the side of the road.

My body started shaking as the tears turned into a geyser. Then a current of strength began to swell. A power activated deep inside me. The wave of emotion passed. All the anxiety that I had been rolling around in dissolved.

For the remainder of the trip I felt peaceful. An energy of commitment to my essence gently pulsed from my core. I wondered how long I would be able to hold this lovely, high vibe. I drove into Santa Barbara at two in the morning, tired, calm, and happy to be home.

The next morning I woke at 10:00 to the sounds of rain on the tin roof of the one-bedroom cottage I was renting from a friend. The anxiety started to creep back in; I felt a surge of desire for Andrew swell up inside me. Instead of focusing on my divine line and pulling all my commitment, expectations, attachment, and desire nuggets off Andrew, I picked up the phone and called him. He picked up on the second ring. "Hi, Aleya, how was your trip?"

Shocked that he was actually on the line, I successfully fell all over myself in a heartbeat. All the work I had done the day before went down the drain. I was lost again in the land of Andrew.

In a cheerful and overly hopeful voice I said, "It was great, but I am really happy to be back, and I would love to see you."

"Um, Aleya, I have to tell you something. Can you come over this morning?"

The ten-minute drive felt like it took forever. The guides had not been wrong. My Higher Self had gotten the right information. Ugh. The words "This relationship that never was will never be" repeated over and over in my head.

My mind and heart started to prepare for the hit and the dump. *I knew that he was not my lifelong partner, but why couldn't it have lasted a little longer? He was so handsome,* I silently whined.

A thousand years later, in five minutes, I knocked on Andrew's door. I walked into his tiny apartment, feeling like I was about to pass out. I began my silent mantra, "It's all right. Commit to the light that runs within you."

"Come on in, Aleya. You should probably sit down." He guided me to his 1950s couch, which was covered in horrendous fabric and had no cushions left to speak of. He began, "I can't believe it, but the day after you left town, my ex-girlfriend contacted me. We talked for a long time, and we are going to try to make it work this time."

I swallowed my instant enlightenment pill and replied, "That's so wonderful. I hope the two of you will be happy together. Thank you for your courage and for being honest and open with me."

He was stunned. I got up and walked to my car. I drove a mile and started bawling. I couldn't stop. I was like a little baby who cries so hard it seems like it's going to die or at least heave up a lung. It was a deep grief that I did not even know I possessed.

After an hour of uncontrollable crying, I found myself seventy miles up the coast near Arroyo Grande. I drove and cried, cried and drove. All along, the thoughts and feelings of betrayal, and injustice, washed over me. The deepest hurt was his inability to be faithful to this new love — me — that he had just found!

As I cried the Niagara Falls of tears, I asked how this could have happened to me. The words of my guides the day before began to hit me more deeply as I swallowed the reality of being dumped. I decided that opening my ears and heart to my guides and Team might be a wise idea.

I pulled over onto a scenic overlook and turned off my car. The sound of the waves quieted me down a little. I felt my guides and Team slowly gathering around me. I could hear their quiet words between the waves. "Where inside are you not faithful and committed to yourself?" they asked.

I closed my eyes, took a breath, increased my courage, and delved deep within. *"Where am I holding back from committing to myself?"*

As I explored my inner world, I was guided through a helpful process, which I will share with you here. This protocol will help you boost your inner commitment quotient. As you increase your commitment to your own essence, you will feel more confident and will create fewer situations of betrayal, rejection, and abandonment.

Growing Your Inner Commitment

Use your imagination, intent, and Higher Self to drop deep inside. Pull your awareness into your divine line. Ask yourself, "Where am I holding back from committing deeply to my essence, that divine part of me?" You may feel as if there is an empty hole inside you. You may feel fear, insecurity, abandonment, or a deep sense of disconnection.

Take a deep breath, and imagine your divine line on the front of your spine. Pull yourself deeper and deeper into this inner river of light, using your breath and your intent.

When you push yourself deeper inside, fear may rise up. I invite you to hold a fierce determination to commit and to connect even more deeply to your inner light as you push deeper. Your determination will help propel you through the waves of fear until they subside.

Now say, "*I ask the Higher Selves of me, my body deva, and my Team to work with the energetic fields and the guides to pull all our awareness into our own divine lines. We ask that all energy nuggets of commitment be located. We ask that all vibrations of commitment to our own divine light be held appropriately in the divine lines of me, my body deva, and Team.*"

Ask your guides and the Ascended Masters to hold a deep connection and commitment to their essence and to model that to you, your body deva, and your Team at the level of their Higher Selves.

Take a moment and imagine standing in your inner river of light. Imagine holding all your commitment nuggets in your divine line. Imagine your body deva holding all its commitment nuggets in its divine line, which runs in the spine. Invite your Team to do the same.

What does it feel like to commit to your essence before anything else? You may feel a calm current and lightness flowing inside you. Your shoulders may relax as your Higher Self and Team members hold this deeper level of inner commitment as well.

RESPONSIBILITY TO SELF

When I used this process after the Andrew moment, the sharp edge of rejection receded. Every time I felt the pain surge up, I increased my commitment and connection to my essence. Within a few months I could think of him not as a jerk but as a tool for learning a huge lesson about committing more deeply to myself. Now when I see him around town with one of his multiple ex-girlfriends, my heart is calm, and I wonder what I ever saw in him in the first place.

My experience with Andrew was a painful way to learn that

my internal lack of commitment created a situation in which another could not commit to me. I had to swallow the reality that somewhere deep inside I was not completely committing to my essence and was essentially betraying myself.

As soon as I acknowledged this fact, I was empowered to change it. I used my Higher Self, my energy fields (the flow of energy that surrounds me and reflects the energy I hold inside and in the higher realms), my intent, and the assistance of the guides to help me locate where I had not fully committed to myself. I then increased my commitment to my essence.

This has continued to be a process. Each day I pull myself into my divine line and increase my connection and commitment to my light. I have discovered that the more I commit to myself, the more others commit to me.

Life is an amazing indicator and reflector. It shows you that what you hold inside is created in your outer world. As we know, you can only change something if you are aware of it. The physical realm can help you become aware of your internal reality. As I unpacked this concept, I discovered a certain level of resistance around the idea that I was the creator of my own reality. As I delved deeper, I realized that not taking responsibility for my life and what I create was putting me in the victim seat.

As soon as you take responsibility, you will stop being a victim. It may not be easy, but it is far more pleasant than living life as the injured party. As soon as you can proclaim, "I am the creator of my own reality," you will be in the boot camp of personal responsibility. At first this may be daunting, but the more you explore this stance, the more you will realize that you are not responsible for anyone else's reality but your own. For years, you may have been walking around holding responsibility for and attachment to other people's journeys. This can be exhausting.

In the past, when I took responsibility for other people's lives,

I was essentially saying to them that I did not think they had the wisdom or capacity to handle their own journey. Was this arrogant and disempowering? Yes. I slowly realized that this pattern did not serve others or me.

When you hold responsibility for cultivating, connecting, and amplifying your inner light, your life will become much more enjoyable. You will hold a higher vibration, model a healthier energy to others, and be of greater service.

INCREASING CONNECTION

After Andrew, I spent a lot of time focusing on the light that flowed in my divine line. The more I focused on this inner light, the stronger it became. As it amplified within me, I was able to recognize the unique qualities that flowed in this inner river.

When you spend time in meditation focusing on the light flowing in your divine line, you cultivate a deeper appreciation for this light. This, in turn, increases self-love. When you begin to look internally for connection and love, you will find it.

So how do we do this? Let's take a moment to increase self-love and your connection to your divine light. You can make the following requests silently or out loud. Remember to pause after each request and let it happen in the higher realms.

ACTIVATING SELF-LOVE AND CONNECTION IN YOUR DIVINE LINE

"I ask the Higher Selves of me, my body deva, and my Team to work with the energetic fields and the guides to lift all our reference points for connection and love off of everyone and everything and to bring them back to our divine lines.

"I ask for the vibration of self-love and connection to activate in our divine lines."

Take a deep breath in, and pull yourself into your divine line. Explore the vibrations flowing in your inner river. Imagine a current of self-love and connection flowing there. The only thing you need to love and connect with is your inner river of light, which is perfect and whole (a little sip from the Seventh Cup).

MANIFESTING A BELOVED PARTNER

You may be looking for a beloved partner, or you may already be in a relationship but want more intimacy. You may be yearning for a deeper sense of connection inside yourself. You might want to feel more love and less self-judgment. As you shift your inner relationship, your outer relationships will change as well.

It took me three years to find my beloved partner. I rolled up my sleeves and became a bulldog with a bone. I focused intently on cultivating a more loving and deeper connection to my essence. When I felt a desire for an intimate partner, I directed this yearning internally. I used this redirected yearning to push myself deep inside my divine line and find a deeper self-love and connection to my essence. The more I did so, the closer I got to manifesting my beloved partner.

One morning my assistant, Ashley, cheerfully greeted me as I walked into my office in Fresno, where I was seeing clients. "Hi, Aleya. You're fully booked all day, and your 12:00 client is a 'potential.' I've known him for several years. I gave him a psychic reading a few years ago, and I think you were in it."

"What? Really?" I was breathless and, at the same time, doubtful.

Every time I thought that a person I was about to meet was a potential beloved partner, I would get my hopes up. So if Superman on enlightenment steroids did not walk through the door, I was devastated. That wave of disappointment could last for weeks. It could also dampen my quest for months at a time. After the last cold spell, I vowed to not get my hopes up, stay in the present moment, and maintain my connection to my essence.

I took a deep breath and calmed myself. "Thanks for the heads-up, Ashley."

I thought to myself, "Maybe he is a potential partner, maybe he isn't. We shall see."

I used every ounce of energy to stay in the present moment and increase my connection to my inner light. My pulse slowed, and my breath came back to a balanced rhythm. Every time I felt myself slip into the future, I would pull myself back into the present breath of now. I had successfully attained a state of inner calm and nonattachment.

Now for a little backstory. I had been dreaming about a particular man for three years. In the higher realms, I could feel his vibration and hear the sound of his Soul. Every person has a unique light and sound that flows in his or her divine line. It creates an energetic signature, similar to a fingerprint. And after my enlightenment moment on the sound table, I was able to energetically see and hear the unique fingerprint of each individual I connected with in the physical realm and in the higher realms.

I would joke with my clairvoyant friends that I was dimensionally dating this mystery man. I had energetically shared his light signature with them and asked that, if they found him, they send him in. Well, today one of my friends had done just that.

Noon rolled around, and he walked into my office. I looked up and, keeping my professional stance, introduced myself. I invited him to take a seat. I explained the process and asked what his intentions were for the session. When he climbed up on the table, I placed my hands on his feet. I felt pulses of energy running through my body and his. These pulses were stronger than usual, but I was trying my best not to read anything into it.

I cleared my mind, pulled myself into my divine line, traveled up to my Higher Self, and connected to his Higher Self. I scanned his fields to see what energy his Higher Self wanted to embody. During the first few words of the first protocol, he drifted off. His energy fields came online as his mind went offline.

I held space for his Higher Self to work. His heart chakra opened, and vibrations of trust, clarity, and courage began to emanate from him in the higher realms.

As his heart opened, I saw his light signature.

I took a deep breath in and checked the light signature of the man I had been dreaming about. It was a match!

For a moment, I felt faint as all the blood rushed to my head. My guides swooped in and helped me stabilize. The fact that this man was a match was a shock and a relief — and very frightening. He was actually real!

I took a deep breath and said to myself, "No big deal. The man I have been tracking in the higher realms for three years is now lying on my table."

I had learned enough about men to know that I could not just kneel down and tell him that he was my beloved lifelong partner and ask if we could we sail off into the sunset together at 5:00 PM after my last client. I had to be incredibly conscious and patient.

The guides took over and worked with him in the higher realms. While they finished the work, I used every bit of power to pull myself into the present moment, access a vibration of self-love, and connect deeply to my own essence.

I completed his sound-healing session with tuning forks and asked him how he felt.

"Wow. I feel really happy. My heart feels really open," he said, still groggy.

As he stood up to go, I took a deep breath and said, "It has been an honor to work with you, but I can never see you professionally again."

He furrowed his brow. "Why?"

"Time will tell, but if you ever want to come to Santa Barbara and go kayaking, let me know."

He smiled and said, "I have your number, and you have mine."

As he walked down the hall, I thought to myself, "Well, I found him."

For me to draw in a potential beloved partner, I had to hold the vibration of connection and self-love in my divine line. The more I connected with my own essence and loved that part of me, the more I drew him in. My inner connection and self-love had acted as a big magnet.

MEETING YOUR OWN NEEDS

One of the most challenging aspects of being in a relationship with another is taking responsibility for meeting your own needs. If you ask the other person to meet them, you will quickly wade into the waters of codependence.

If I want you to validate and approve of me, I am not meeting that need inside myself. It is a disempowering experience. When I hold responsibility for validating and approving of my inner light, I do not need those things from you. I will then be able to show up in the relationship feeling less needy. I will be more secure and supported inside myself and able to hold a safer and more supported space for you, in a healthy way.

When you ask and depend on others to love, appreciate, approve, and validate you, you are essentially looking externally for your needs to be met instead of meeting them for yourself. If others do not love or approve of you in the ways you desire, you will feel disappointed, frustrated, and unsupported.

The more you meet your needs internally, the more abundant your life will be. You will also create and sustain healthier relationships. This is empowering and fulfilling for everyone involved.

I invite you to take a moment and retrieve all responsibility for supporting yourself. Here's how.

RETRIEVING RESPONSIBILITY

Ask your Higher Self, your body deva, and your Team to retrieve all the responsibility you gave to others for supporting you. Hold that responsibility in the divine lines of you, your body deva, and your Team. Ask for the vibration of support to activate in the divine lines of you, your body deva, and your Team.

Take a moment, and wait for those vibrations to reflect from the higher realms into this one. Imagine and feel the vibration of support flowing in your divine line, like a stream of light. You just met your own needs. How easy.

TURNING IT BACK TO YOU

When you want to effect change in your life, focus on shifting the energy inside yourself. Hold the vibration of what you want in your outer life in your divine line and at the level of your Higher Self. Ask your body deva and your Team to hold these same qualities in their divine lines and at the level of their Higher Selves. Remember the sacred trinity. When you use all three of these energies — you, your body deva, and your Team — amazing things happen.

Six months into my relationship with Doug, I was standing at the kitchen sink doing the dinner dishes. As I stood there, scrubbing a plate, I had a desire for him to appreciate me and all that

I did for him. As soon as I felt that desire, I felt a little swirl of energy coming from my guides and Team and heard their wise words drifting down to me: "Meet that need inside yourself."

So I took a moment to practice the deeper layers of the Third Cup. I took a deep breath in, closed my eyes, and brought my awareness into my divine line. From that place, I asked my Higher Self to activate the vibration of self-appreciation. I held a gentle awareness as my Higher Self spun the energy of appreciation for my essence within and around me.

A moment later, I felt waves of self-appreciation flow inside me and wrap around me like a warm blanket. I kept washing the dishes and checked my outer desire for Doug to appreciate me. It was gone. A few minutes later, he came into the kitchen and, wrapping his arms around my waist, whispered in my ear, "I really appreciate you and all that you do for me."

I was stunned. After six months of meeting my own needs, this was one of the first times it had been reflected back to me so quickly and clearly. It was like magic! Except it had required a bit of conscious and energetic work to get there.

The even stranger thing was that, in that moment, I didn't *need* his appreciation. It was nice, but it was more of a reflection of my inner state. As he embraced me, I realized that had I not done the work a few moments before, I would be desperately slurping up his appreciation. But there was no slurping, just a deep inner confirmation. I was able to receive his appreciation only to the degree that I had received my own. I felt empowered and full instead of needy, empty, and wanting more.

As you sip from the Third Cup, you may begin to notice a greater sense of peace and inner contentment. You might also notice that you do not use your energy trying to change other people and how they act; you use it on yourself. Your focus may be more directed toward cultivating very particular qualities in your divine line, as opposed to holding your awareness solely on your outer world. As you make these inner shifts, they will begin to reflect into your physical life, and your relationships with others will become less strained and more fulfilling.

Insights and Things to Remember

- Your internal reality reflects into your outer world.
- If you wish to change your outer life, you must become aware of your internal environment by observing your emotions and behavior.
- You can use your external reality to help you determine the energy you are holding internally. If you do not feel supported in your outer life, use that awareness to increase inner support. As you cultivate greater inner support, it will inevitably reflect in your outer life.
- Hold all attachment and desire for your own internal reality and no one else's.
- Swallow the pill...take responsibility for your own emotions and internal energy.
- Before making a request, pull your awareness into your divine line. Get "online" to make a request to your Higher Self.
- Use your Higher Self to activate the energy you desire in your divine line and at the level of your Higher Self, and wait for the reflection.
- The more awareness you hold internally, the greater the reflection becomes; that is, your consciousness will amplify the vibrations you are holding in your divine line and create a reflection.
- Remember that the outer world is the mirror of your inner world.
- Change your inner life, and your outer life will reflect those inner changes.

The How

Ready to make some inner changes? Let's dive into the spiritual lab and practice the quick steps for changing your outer world by changing your inner world. Then we'll practice the full protocol for taking responsibility and shifting your inner energy.

The Quick Steps

What aspect of your life would you like to change? The balance in your bank account? Your intimate relationship? The way people treat you? Identify your need. Do you desire greater support, respect, or appreciation? Retrieve all responsibility for meeting that need. It is no one else's job to support you, respect you, or appreciate you. When you hold responsibility for meeting this need energetically inside yourself, you move into greater empowerment, fulfillment, and abundance. Using your Higher Self and energy fields, activate the vibration of this need at the level of your Higher Self and in your divine line. When you invite your Higher Self to shift the vibrations in the higher realms, those shifts will be reflected into your physical reality.

As you work through the full protocol below, you can read the sentences in italics silently or out loud — whatever feels right for you.

The Full Protocol

1. Identify the energy or emotion inside you that you would like to shift. You can use your outer world to help you determine the appropriate vibration. (Example: If you want

connection or happiness in your life, activate the vibration of connection or happiness in your divine line.)

2. Bring your awareness into your divine line using your breath, imagination, intent, and Higher Self: *"I ask my Higher Self to work with my energetic fields and the guides to bring all my awareness into my divine line."* Stand in your inner column of light.

3. *"I ask my Higher Self to retrieve all responsibility for (my happiness, supporting myself, respecting myself, protecting myself, and so on)."* Imagine your Higher Self gathering all responsibilities for meeting this particular need.

4. *"I ask my Higher Self to retrieve and hold all my gifts, wisdom, and mastery for meeting that need."* Feel, imagine, and intend holding all your responsibility and ability for meeting that need in yourself.

5. *"I invite my Higher Self to work with my energetic fields and the guides to activate the vibration of (support, respect, appreciation, value, and so on) at the level of my Higher Self and in my divine line."* Take a deep breath in, and imagine holding your awareness in your divine line. Hold awareness that your Higher Self is activating the intended vibration and retrieving all the responsibilities that are yours for meeting that need. You can imagine that your Higher Self has a cosmic vacuum cleaner and is sucking all energetic responsibilities back to you at the level of your Higher Self. This is the part where you sprinkle the ingredients of faith and magic, and wait. Let your Higher Self do the work. If you sense that your Higher Self does not know how, ask the guides to help. Ask them to model the "how" to your Higher Self and to send the appropriate information to you, wherever you have the capacity to receive it.

6. Imagine a stream of energy flowing in your divine line that carries the particular vibration you are intending on embodying and then creating/reflecting into your outer world. For example, imagine a stream of inner peace, support, love, or connection flowing inside you.

7. Take a deep breath. Move into appreciation for this inner current of energy. Allow, acknowledge, and embrace the vibration(s) that are flowing inside you. Hold the awareness that this inner energy will inevitably be reflected back to you in your outer world.

8. As you hold the awareness of this energy flowing inside you, invite all your reference points and ways of perceiving and being perceived to be updated. Tap and reset your energetic fuel gauge: *"I invite my Higher Self to update all my reference points and all ways of perceiving and being perceived."*

9. You are complete. As you sleep, dream, and play, keep holding a gentle awareness that your Higher Self is activating these particular vibrations in the higher realms as well as in your divine line. This energy is reflecting down to you in the physical realm.

THIRD CUP AUDIO MEDITATION

To listen to the audio meditation for the Third Cup, go to www.cupsofconsciousness.com/meditations.

Activating Your Desired Vibrations in Your Divine Line

This meditation guides you through the following process: Think of the energy you would like to have in your outer life. Invite your Higher Self to retrieve and hold all your attachment, desire, and responsibility for embodying those vibrations in your divine line. Invite your Higher Self, your body deva, and your Team to activate and hold that vibration in your own divine lines. Perceive that vibration flowing in the divine lines of you, your body deva, and your Team. As you hold that conscious awareness of that inner energy, invite this vibration to reflect into your outer world.

May your inner joy, connection, support,
and love reflect back to you in your outer world.

FOURTH CUP

Your Challenges Can Help You Grow

> **Every challenge is an opportunity to accelerate your growth and evolution.**

*L*ife is filled with peaks and valleys. The trick is knowing how to move through the valleys without getting stuck in the mud, and how to use the peaks to carry you through the next valley.

Challenges — breakups, illnesses, deaths, job changes, inner sadness, frustration, and so on — can be very uncomfortable experiences. The good news is that you can use discomfort to awaken. As mentioned in the last chapter, awareness creates the capacity to change by allowing you to take responsibility for your internal reality. Now add the Fourth Cup to the equation, and realize that most people do the opposite of what they are attempting to master. This might sound crazy and inefficient, and yes, it is. Yet most people do just that until they've had enough.

Imagine being determined to master empowerment. You may play the role of the victim over and over until you reach your breaking point. When you have had enough, you flip your challenge and embody the solution by attaining the vibration of empowerment.

Every challenge in life has a "flip it," a solution. The trick is to recognize the challenge and figure out the remedy. When you can consciously flip your challenges, amazing changes will take place.

In short, you use the challenges in your outer world to determine what is going on energetically. Then you use protocols to make the necessary energetic changes within yourself, your body deva, and your Team. As the energetic changes take effect, you will experience fewer challenges, and you will begin taking responsibility for attaining the qualities you are determined to master.

The process for flipping your challenges can be distilled into three steps:

1. Discern it.
2. Flip it.
3. Observe it.

Think of a challenge you are facing. Perhaps it is the low balance in your bank account. Maybe it's the way someone treats you, or the way you treat yourself, or a particular behavior of yours that you dislike. Maybe it's your lack of motivation and discipline to eat well and exercise.

Why are you being challenged in this way? What are you attempting to learn? Determine the nature of the challenge. Think of it as an opportunity to become stronger, healthier, and happier.

As you no doubt have experienced, willpower and good intentions aren't always enough. The secret is using your Higher Self to activate the solution. When you ask your Higher Self to do the work, your challenge transforms into your greatest strength. Your struggle becomes an enlightenment moment.

DISCERNING YOUR CHALLENGES

You might spend several weeks discerning the root of your challenge and the solution. I find that journaling is helpful in this process. Write out basic questions, and answer them with stream-of-consciousness writing. Write down every thought that comes into your awareness, with no censoring. Allow your unconscious to have a voice.

Identify one challenge you want to shift. (Go with something small for now; don't pick your biggest challenge. Once you learn these steps, you can work on bigger challenges.) What are you trying to learn with this challenging situation? How would you feel if you got it? What needs would be met? Do you need safety? Respect? Connection? Support? Love?

Discerning your challenges can be difficult because, after all, you are enmeshed in them. The secret to discerning the nature of a challenge is to become aware of the emotions around the challenge. Your emotions can help you identify your needs and find the solution.

Here's how to do it.

IDENTIFYING THE EMOTIONS BEHIND THE CHALLENGE

Identify the first emotion you feel when you think about your challenge. Really let yourself feel it. Is there another emotion underneath it? Look for the deepest emotional charge. This is when courage comes in handy.

Your most obvious emotion might be anger. Under the anger may be grief. Underneath the grief may be loss. Underneath the loss may be fear. When you reach fear, you may feel a huge charge. If so, then you know that fear is the root of your challenge. The root emotion is always more charged than the emotions that came before it.

Ride your emotions as a surfer rides waves. Think of emotions as energy in motion: e-motion. Use them to propel you deeper to find the root. Try not to identify with your emotions. Just let them roll through you. The more you surrender to these waves of energy, the more quickly they will pass. Let your body deva experience the emotion with tears, laughter, shaking, or whatever expression it chooses.

You can also use these waves of energy to move you forward and up into a higher vibration. If you feel a wave of fear when you think about the balance in your bank account, imagine riding the wave of fear into the vibration of trust, support, and flow. Surf the wave forward and up to higher ground. Ask your Higher Self to activate the vibration of support, trust, and flow in your divine line. Your fear of lack will dissolve. Over time, you will reflect your inner support in your outer world.

As soon as you feel the deepest emotional charge, move to the next step: flip it.

Think of the challenge you would like to transform. Struggle, lack, fear? What is the solution to this challenge? Flow? Abundance? Empowerment? Trust? Remember, you are determined to acquire particular qualities. What do you value or desire?

You can use the resources in the Flip-It section later in this chapter to help you determine the solution to your challenge. You may also visit my online resource page at www.cupsofconscious ness.com/meditations, where you will find the full Flip-It list.

When you are ready to flip your challenge into the solution, use your Higher Self to activate the vibration of the solution. Your challenge will transform into your greatest strength. The specific protocol for flipping a challenge into the solution is this: *"I invite the Higher Selves of me, my body deva, and my Team to work with the energetic fields and the guides to activate the vibration and mechanisms of the solution and flip my challenge into my greatest strength."*

Here's a quick summary of the process:

1. Identify the challenge. (Someone disrespected you.)
2. How do you feel? (You are angry.)
3. What do you need? (You want to be respected.)
4. The solution: Hold responsibility for respecting yourself, and activate the vibration of respect in your divine line. Respect yourself. Let go of needing someone else to respect you.

After you have invited your Higher Self to activate the vibration of the solution, observe. Take a deep breath, and sit like a bump on a log. Hold awareness, and imagine the Higher Selves of you, your body deva, and your Team doing the work in the higher realms. After waiting for a minute or two, you might feel the energy shifting. It may feel like little waves rolling in from the higher realms. When I do this for myself, I sometimes feel a deep sense of relief that brings tears or laughter.

You may feel the shift in a few seconds, minutes, hours, or weeks. It depends on the size of your request. The bigger the request, the longer it may take for it to reflect into the physical realm. When I became clear about my desire for a life partner, for example, it took me a few years before I found him in the physical realm. When I wanted to shift my financial struggles, it took about three years. Be patient and persistent.

When you embrace your challenges as opportunities for growth and evolution, your life starts moving forward in an empowering and magical way.

TAKING FINANCIAL RESPONSIBILITY AND PULLING UP MY BOOTSTRAPS

The process of discerning, shifting, and observing can be subtle or dramatic. It might take you a day, a month, or a year to shift your challenges and practice what you wish to master.

As always, I learned this concept the hard way.

My cell phone rang while I was standing in line for my two-shot cappuccino at a coffee shop in Portland, Oregon. I was still on my quest to find a new home, road-tripping out of Telluride every three to four weeks.

I stepped out of line, walked outside, and took the call.

"Is this Aleya Dao? This is the Bank of Telluride. We are letting you know that your mortgage check has not yet been deposited. You are five days late, and we are following up with you to see how you would like to handle this situation."

"What? I confirmed with my tenants that they would deposit a check just a few days ago. I will call them and work on remedying this immediately."

My body went into full-on fight-or-flight within seconds. No need for my cappuccino now. I sat in a parking lot feeling lost, angry, unsupported, and freaked out. Losing the house to foreclosure would be disastrous. I should have listened to my gut and not rented my precious house to two people who had struck me as a bit irresponsible.

My hands still shaking, I dialed one of the tenants.

"Scott, this is Aleya. I just got a phone call from the bank saying they have not yet received a check for the mortgage payment."

"Oh, yeah, sorry about that. I have been a little behind, but I will do it today."

"Scott, you said that to me four days ago, and I'm having a hard time believing you. This is the third time this has happened, and I'm really frustrated. If you don't deposit the check today, I think it would be best if you move out within thirty days." I was finally finding a backbone.

"What, no, you can't do that. I do not have anywhere else to go! Aleya, please!" Scott pleaded.

"I don't know, Scott. Just please deposit the check today. Okay?"

I hung up, feeling a mix of hope, doubt, and anxiety. I had no savings. I was following divine guidance from beings who did not live in the physical realm, and I could only hear them in my quietest moments. I had $289.00 left in my bank account, and five more days on the road before I returned to Telluride to work for ten days straight and sleep on my office floor. A landslide of fearful thoughts started cascading, leaving very little breathing room.

"What if I lose my house? What if I have to file bankruptcy? What if I become a total failure? What if I never find a new community and place to live? What if I never find a partner? What if I'm single, unsupported, and alone forever?"

It was time to pull up my bootstraps. I had hit the mother lode of my issues. As I let the waves wash over me, I could feel an angelic army gathering around me in the higher realms. I heard a gentle, soothing choir descending upon me, whispering the lessons and opportunity for growth around issues of support and money. I cranked up my courage to ask some hard questions. This was an opportunity to sit in the driver's seat instead of staying locked in the trunk.

In this moment I took responsibility for my financial life. Fear and anger can be wonderful motivators.

As the angelic realm encircled me, I saw how my attitude around money was one of lack. Lo and behold, lack was exactly what I was creating for myself. I heard my guides speaking to me, "Aleya, take a deep breath, and let yourself feel all the lack you are entrenched in right now. Collect every little lack nugget you can find that is yours, regarding every aspect of lack in your life."

Sometimes their suggestions were not so pleasant. But the guidance always worked, so I was willing to do whatever was needed to get out of this spiral of fear and anxiety.

Using my intent and imagination, I asked my Higher Self to use my energy fields to gather all perceptions and consciousness of lack in my life. I thought about all the areas of my life that felt like not enough. The list quickly became very long. My anxiety mounted, until I heard the next instruction coming in from the higher realms.

"Ask your Higher Self to activate the vibrations, sounds, and energetic shapes of abundance in your divine line and around the energies of lack that you are holding."

I silently made this request to my Higher Self. I was amazed as my anxiety began to lift. I closed my eyes and saw my Higher Self. In a flash of light, I saw that energetic aspect of me weaving an elaborate web of light, sound, and beautiful geometric shapes of abundant energy around all the little and big moments when I had ever felt impoverished.

Suddenly, my anxiety was gone. Completely gone. No sobbing, no whining, no "What am I going to do?" No freak-out. The anxiety was just gone.

That didn't solve the problem with my tenants and the bank, however. What it did do was put me in a better energetic and emotional condition to deal with my physical reality. I felt more attached and supported by my inner flow of abundance, as well as more neutral regarding my outer challenges.

I practiced this technique for six months. The moment fear of lack surfaced, I would use my Higher Self and my Team to activate the vibration of abundance in my divine line. Each time, the fearful emotions would release, and I would feel calm and supported.

For another two years, though I lived on a financial edge, I no longer had an emotional charge around it. Slowly, money started flowing to me, and I stopped living in the poverty consciousness and did not lose my house to foreclosure. After a few more years the fear of lack was a tiny pebble compared to the boulder it used to be. The more you address the layers of your challenges, the smaller they become.

So now I would like to share with you the protocol I developed for moving from poverty to abundance.

MOVING INTO ABUNDANCE

"I invite the Higher Selves of me, my body deva, and my Team to work with the energetic fields and the guides to dissolve all vibrations of lack off all aspects of me, my body deva, and my Team using sacred sounds, light, and vibrations of abundance. I ask for an activation of the vibrations of abundance, flow, and support in the divine lines and at the level of the Higher Selves of me, my body deva, and my Team. We hold the vibrations of support, abundance, trust, and flow as a way of mastering abundance."

Bring your awareness into your divine line. Imagine an inner current of abundance flowing there. Invite your body deva and your Team members to hold their awareness in their divine lines and to embrace those same vibrations.

Every day, be aware that a stream of support and abundance is flowing in your divine line. Feel how you are supported by the light that flows in your divine line. Do this until your outer resources shift. Eventually, the flow of abundance will reflect into your outer life.

A Quick Flip-It Guide

To help you see the process of flipping a challenge more clearly, here is a quick guide showing some challenges and their solutions.

- If you do not feel like there is ever enough, the solution is activating the vibration and consciousness of *abundance.*
- If you are entrenched in fear, the solution is embodying inner *trust, safety, and empowerment.*
- If you feel like a victim, the solution is to master *empowerment.* Find your power in your own divine line. Hold responsibility for cultivating greater power in your divine line.
- If you feel abandoned, attain *connection* by bringing your awareness back to your divine line and feeling connection to your essence.
- If you feel disrespected, you are giving someone responsibility for respecting you. Take back the responsibility for respecting yourself. Increase *self-respect* for the light that flows in your divine line.
- If you have experienced a betrayal, it is an opportunity to increase your *commitment to yourself.*
- If you are feeling depressed, use your Higher Self to pull yourself into your divine line. Ask your Higher Self to activate the vibration of *joy* in your divine line. Find your joy there. Give yourself permission to rest. Unplug. Restore. Go deep into your divine line without having to use the depression energy.

- If you feel hatred for yourself or others, move into *self-love* by cultivating love for the light that flows in your divine line. When you love yourself, you are able to more fully love others.
- If you are in judgment of yourself or others, practice *acceptance* by opening your heart to yourself. Accept and embrace the light that flows in your divine line.
- If you feel lonely, the solution is *connection*. Use your breath to pull yourself into your divine line. Find your connection in your inner river, not in the outer world.
- If you feel rejected and want to be liked and accepted, the solution is *self-acceptance*. The world accepts you to the extent that you accept yourself. Before worrying about what anyone else thinks, accept and approve of the light that flows in your divine line.

This Flip-It list is meant as a guide only. You may come up with solutions that are not on the list. Exploring the qualities of your challenge will always help you find the solution, whatever it may be.

You can use the steps below to master the process of flipping your challenges. At the end of this chapter, you will have an opportunity to practice these steps again with specific requests to the Higher Selves of you, your body deva, and your Team.

FLIPPING YOUR CHALLENGES

1. Think of an upsetting situation: Your neighbor yelled at you. Your partner forgot to text you to tell you he or she would be late for dinner. Your friends never ask about you; it is always about them. You always negatively critique yourself after spending time with others. Whatever

the challenge may be, think of something you would like to change. Let go of any judgment. Let yourself explore the root of your challenge.

2. Ask yourself what you are determined to master by creating and/or engaging in this energy or situation. *(This is the moment when you are moving into the driver's seat. You are acknowledging that, for some reason, you are engaging in this disempowering energy. Instead of being a victim in the situation, you are using the challenge to grow stronger and to move into a more empowered consciousness.)*

3. What internal energy do you want to attain? Empowerment? Trust? Abundance? Connection? Think about the positive side of this challenge. What is the solution? Refer to the Flip-It section online to get the full list.

4. Invite the Higher Selves of you, your body deva, and your Team to locate all the energies and consciousness of the challenge (fear, lack, victim, and so on).

5. Release those mechanisms for mastering the vibration of the solution using sacred shapes, sounds, vibrations, and light.

6. Invite the Higher Selves of you, your body deva, and your Team to activate the grids, vibrations, and consciousness of the solution (safety, abundance, empowerment, connection, and so on) in your divine line and at the level of your Higher Selves.

7. Invite the Higher Selves of you, your body deva, and your Team to take full responsibility for holding this vibration in your divine lines and at the level of your Higher Selves. *(This step is the moment when you take full responsibility for mastering an inner vibration. You are no longer asking the outer world to challenge you. You are using the tool of personal responsibility and practicing what you intend to master instead of doing the opposite.)*

8. Ask for a release of all external challenges and situations as a way of mastering this vibration. You no longer need the outer world to challenge you to grow.

9. Ask your angelic guides and the Ascended Masters to encircle you and model the solution to you, your body deva, and your Team in the higher realms.

10. As you move through your day, hold an awareness of the inner vibration of the solution flowing in your divine line. Imagine your body deva and your Team holding that same vibration inside their divine lines.

When you start to identify your challenges as opportunities, you will stop running from them.

INSIGHTS AND THINGS TO REMEMBER

- You can use the higher dimensions to shift your emotional and physical reality (First Cup). Your inner reality creates your outer world (Third Cup). If you want to shift a challenge, you need to climb into the driver's seat and take responsibility. Use every challenge as an opportunity to grow and evolve and to practice what you intend to master (Fourth Cup).

- Individually and collectively, uncomfortable situations, behaviors, and relationships force people to grow. The more painful the situation, the more intense the awakening and the more determined the Soul is to evolve.

- Every challenge is an opportunity for growth. The only question is whether you will recognize and act on the opportunity. If you don't, you may create another larger, more painful challenge. Flip it, and embrace the vibration of what your Soul is determined to master.

- When you reach a certain level of self-awareness, you will begin to practice what you wish to master. To master empowerment, you will hold the vibration of empowerment in your divine line.

- Increase your courage, look deep within, and flip your challenge.
- Address the need that is being met by the challenging behavior or situation. You may be using anxiety and fear to protect yourself, keeping yourself on guard and in a high state of alert. Instead use your Higher Self and energy fields to protect yourself. Release the on-guard fear stance.
- Use your emotions as fuel. Imagine surfing your emotions as if they were waves. Propel yourself forward and up into a higher vibration and consciousness.
- Ask your Higher Self to use all the energy of the challenge and flip it to the vibration your Soul is determined to attain.
- If your challenge does not shift, ponder the possibility that you are holding an issue that does not belong to you, your body deva, or your Team. Using your Higher Self, send the challenge back to its right and perfect place, along with all appropriate information.
- Take responsibility only for your own emotions and challenges.
- Hold compassion and a loving space for other people to have their own emotions and challenges. Their challenges are like the weights they are lifting at the gym; they are helping them grow stronger.

The How

Whatever the challenge is, you can always unpack it, and then flip it, by asking yourself the following questions: (1) Why has my Soul consciously or unconsciously created this situation? (2)

What am I attempting to learn? (Refer to the Flip-It section online.) (3) What need is being addressed? What if I consciously practiced the behavior I am attempting to master instead of doing the opposite?

Let's dive into the spiritual lab now, where we can practice the quick steps and the more detailed protocol to help you use your challenges to evolve. You can also listen to the audio meditation at the end of this chapter.

THE QUICK STEPS

Identify the challenge. Think of the solution or the opposite. (Refer to the full Flip-It section online.) Use your breath, awareness, Higher Self, and energy fields to pull yourself into your divine line. While holding your awareness in your divine line, send your request to your Higher Self. Invite your Higher Self to energetically locate the unhealthy behavior or attitude that you want to shift. Wait a moment while your Higher Self locates that energy.

Invite your Higher Self to transform these lower vibrations into the vibration of what you are attempting to master. Invite your Higher Self to create and activate grids, templates, blueprints, and a way of being that holds the solution. Invite your Higher Self to activate the vibration of the solution in your divine line. Imagine your Higher Self embodying the solution and/or engaging in this healthier behavior in a higher realm.

Invite your Higher Self to reflect the solution to you in the physical realm. Invite your body deva and your Team to transform the vibration of the challenge into the solution as well. Ask them to hold the vibration of the solution at the level of their Higher Selves and in their own divine lines. Update all your reference points and all the ways in which you perceive and are perceived in the world. Check your emotional charge around the behavior or challenge. Did it shift a lot or a little?

Do not expect instantaneous results. How long have you held this belief, attitude, or behavior? The longer you have held a particular energy, the more layered it can be. You may need to spend some time working through all the layers before your challenge flips completely, so be patient.

THE FULL PROTOCOL

1. Identify the challenge.
2. Go digging, and find the root of the issue. Increase courage. Take time to identify the core issue.
3. What is the challenging behavior? Feeling fear? Lack? Abandonment? What are your feelings regarding this situation? What is the biggest, deepest, most challenging emotion regarding this situation? What is the most challenging aspect that is getting you triggered? What need is not being addressed in this situation? *Every person has a core need for connection, love, approval, respect, safety, trust, and support.*
4. Find the solution, and flip it into the vibration you are determined to master. Think of the solution. Let's say the challenge is feeling that no one values you. You want others to value you, but you are not valuing yourself. You have given all the responsibility of being valued to other people. You have found the root of the challenge. The challenge is not feeling valued and issues of self-worth. The solution is to hold the vibration of self-worth in direct connection with the light that flows in your divine

line. *Feel your self-worth in your divine line.* Follow the emotions, not the line of reason. They will lead you into the deepest piece that is ready to shift.

5. Use your breath, awareness, Higher Self, and energy fields to pull yourself into your divine line on the front of your spine. (Get online when you want to make a request.) You can stay in your divine line on the front of your spine, or you can travel up your divine line to the level of your Higher Self. Either way works. Make the following request silently or out loud: *"I invite my Higher Self to work with my energetic fields and the guides to energetically locate all the vibrations, energy, behaviors, thought forms, grids, and templates that hold the vibration of my challenge (fear, loneliness, lack, and so on)."* Take a moment, and hold an awareness as the energetic aspect of you in a higher realm locates your challenge.

6. Invite your Higher Self to flip these vibrations into the vibration your Soul is determined to master. *"I invite my Higher Self to work with my energetic fields and the guides to bring in sacred shapes, sounds, and light to transform these vibrations of (name the challenge) into the solution of (name the solution)."* Take a moment, and imagine your Higher Self doing this work in the higher realms. You can also imagine the guides helping this aspect of you fully transform the vibrations that have been challenging you into the vibration of the solution.

7. Invite your Higher Self to create vibrations, grids, templates, and blueprints that embody the solution. Hold a more evolved, connected, and empowered way of being: *"I invite my Higher Self to work with my energetic fields and the guides to create and activate the templates, sacred*

shapes, grids, sounds, emotions, and thought forms hold-ing the consciousness of (the solution.)" You do not have to use all the recommendations above. Pick and choose the mechanisms that resonate for you. If you love working with sound, you can ask for the sounds and templates of the solution to support you in holding this more evolved and empowered way of being. The most important as-pect of the activation process is that your Higher Self is creating and activating the vibration of the solution. You are only using your mind to make the request. Imagine and allow that dimensional aspect of you weaving a new way of being in the higher realms. Let this challenge be your greatest strength as it transforms into the vibration of the solution.

8. Invite your Higher Self to embody the solution: *"I invite my Higher Self to fully activate and embody the vibration of (the solution) in my divine line and at the level of my Higher Self."* Imagine your Higher Self engaging in this healthier vibration and behavior in a higher realm.

9. Invite your Higher Self to reflect this energy to you: *"I ask my Higher Self to reflect these vibrations to me here in this physical realm."*

10. Invite your body deva and your Team to do the same: *"I invite the Higher Selves of my body deva and my Team members to work with their energetic fields and the guides to release all energy of (the challenge). I invite my body deva and my Team to bring in and activate the vibrations of (the solution)."* Hold space for your body deva and Team to do this work. Imagine them embodying the healthy behavior and holding the vibration of the solution in their own divine lines.

11. Update all reference points: *"I ask that all the reference*

points for me, my body deva, and my Team be updated, as well as all ways in which we perceive and are perceived." Reset your fuel gauge.

12. Check your emotional charge around the behavior or external situation. Are you more neutral? Is there still a charge? Has it decreased?

As you identify and activate the vibration of the solution, you will release the challenge. At first, your reactivity will diminish. Next, you will be neutral when a challenge arises. Finally, the vibration you are holding inside will transform into the solution. *You will create situations that reflect your inner vibration.*

FOURTH CUP AUDIO MEDITATION

To listen to the audio meditation for the Fourth Cup, go to www .cupsofconsciousness.com/meditations.

Using Your Challenges to Grow

This meditation helps you identify your challenge. First determine the solution to the challenge. Invite the Higher Selves of you, your body deva, and your Team to transform the challenging energy or behavior into the solution; activate the consciousness, emotions, thoughts, and behavior of the solution in your divine lines and at the level of the Higher Selves of you, your body deva, and your Team. Imagine and invite those energetic aspects to fully embody the solution in the higher realms and to reflect that energy to you.

MORE RESOURCES

For the full Flip-It list, visit my webpage for the audio meditations, then click "Other Resources." While you're there, you can also watch my YouTube video "8th Conscious Conversation," which includes advice on learning how to surf the waves of emotion.

Every challenging moment becomes
an opportunity for growth and evolution.
Practice what you intend to master.
Happy flipping!

FIFTH CUP

Your Body Is a Nature Spirit

> **You are not your body.**

Your physical body is a conscious, sentient being that is from Earth. Throughout this book, I refer to your human body as a body deva (*deva* means "nature being"). Your body has a consciousness and energetic fields separate from yours. It also has its own energetic divine line flowing within the spinal cord. Your body deva's divine line contains the essence of itself. It also has a Higher Self, similar to your Higher Self. Your body deva can use its Higher Self and its energetic fields to shift its energy in the higher realms, which in turn reflects into its physical form.

Because you are experiencing life on the physical plane, you may easily confuse yourself with your body deva. It may seem as if there is no difference between you and your form. However, as you awaken, the distinction becomes clearer and clearer.

When you fully realize that you are not your body, magical things happen.

The best way to experience the difference between your consciousness and the consciousness of your body is to connect with your body deva. Here is the protocol for doing just that.

Connecting with Your Body Deva

Take a deep breath in. Pull all your awareness into your divine line, and firmly attach your divine line to the front of your spine. Travel up to your Higher Self. Ask your Higher Self to connect with your body deva's Higher Self: *"I ask my Higher Self to connect with my body deva's Higher Self from a place of love and clarity."* Take a moment to let this happen in the higher realms.

Imagine saying hi to your body deva. Hold a very quiet space. Invite your body deva to acknowledge its own consciousness. Hold your awareness at the level of your Higher Self in your divine line. Imagine your Higher Self locating and connecting with the energetic aspect of your body deva. Imagine lines of love connecting your Higher Self and your body deva's Higher Self.

Holding Space for Your Body Deva

When you connect with your body deva, it might take a few tries before you get a response. Your body deva might be shy when you acknowledge its consciousness for the first time. It took me several years to clearly see my body deva nature spirit.

The first time I ever saw the energetic aspect of my body deva was while on a hike one afternoon. I asked my Higher Self to activate the vibration of self-love in my divine line. Within a few minutes, I felt a sweet warm current flow up and down the front of my spine. I traveled up to my Higher Self and made the request: "I ask my Higher Self to connect with my body deva's Higher Self." As I held my awareness in the higher realm, I saw and felt my body deva's energetic self. I looked at her closely. She had a human form but was composed of light. I could feel an earthly energy emanating from her. To see the energetic aspect of my body deva for the first time was amazing, validating, and comforting. I truly was different from my body.

I acknowledged her and held a quiet space for her to communicate with me if she wished.

After a few moments, she turned to me and said, "I hate you."

I was startled but managed to keep my presence of mind. I asked, "Do you love yourself?"

She turned her back, shook her head, and said, "I want you to love me the way you love yourself."

I asked her, "What if you love yourself to the degree that I love myself, and we reflected that on each other?"

When she told me she didn't know how, I offered to show her. I invited my Higher Self to hold the vibration of self-love at the level of my Higher Self and in my divine line and to model that energy to the Higher Self of my body deva. I asked that any responsibility I might be holding for loving my body be returned to her at the level of her Higher Self. I continued to model the energy of self-love to her for a few more minutes.

I brought my awareness back down into the physical realm. While holding a nonattached stance, I continued to model self-love. After a few minutes, my body deva burst into tears. A huge surge of love began to flow in my spine. She did it!

I thanked my body deva for having the courage to love herself. In the higher realms, I saw her smile, and she thanked me. I opened my eyes and felt a rush of excitement as I reflected on this new connection. It was the breakthrough I had been waiting for.

Your first connection with your body deva might be very different from mine. When your body deva awakens, it may respond in a number of ways. It may feel relief, shame, grief, joy, or anger. Hold space for the release of those emotions. Those are your body deva's emotions, not yours. I learned this through experience.

One evening I felt called to sit in meditation with my body deva. I closed my eyes, took a few conscious breaths, pulled myself into my divine line, and traveled up to my Higher Self.

I asked my guides to encircle me. I asked my Higher Self to connect to my body deva's Higher Self. As my energetic eyes adjusted to this higher plane, I saw a large crystal table, where my guides were seated. I could feel my body deva standing off to the side, so I invited her to sit at the table.

She said, "I feel like I have done something wrong."

I laughed and said, "No, not at all. You did something right! You recognized your own consciousness and had the courage to love yourself."

"I was only able to awaken once you had reached a certain level of consciousness," she said.

Confused, I turned to my guides with questions.

"The Soul that resides in the physical body must reach a certain level of self-awareness and self-love before the body can awaken to a higher level of self-awareness," they said. "When you were on your meadow walk, you were holding that level of self-love. The light of your essence awoke the nature spirit of your physical body."

My guides continued, "Your body is in its own process of evolution, just like you. It is learning to love itself. Its self-awareness increases the more it cultivates self-love and personal responsibility inside its own divine line. Your physical body is a conscious, sentient being."

"What happens if I resist being in the body?" I asked.

"When you resist, you will unconsciously lift your divine line off the front of your spine. Your body deva will experience that withdrawal. It will feel rejected and abandoned, and your health and vitality will deteriorate."

My body deva was crying. I went over to hold her. At first, she pushed me away.

I looked to my guides, who quietly said, "Just hold space for her to have her feelings. Stay near her. Hold a loving safe space for her to be angry or sad. Do not fix her emotions. The body uses emotions to evolve. Let her surf her own waves of emotion."

I held the safest, most loving space for her to feel whatever she needed. As I held this energy inside myself for her, I could feel her heaviness lift.

My guides asked her if she wanted all the moments she had ever felt resistance to be healed. She nodded.

My body deva enveloped herself in multiple orbs of light using her energetic fields. She healed all the moments she ever felt rejected by retrieving responsibility for embracing herself and activating the vibration of connection in her own divine line.

As your body deva recognizes its own consciousness and embraces itself, it becomes stronger, healthier, and happier. It might take a day, a month, or several years to create this healthier reality. The more you acknowledge the consciousness of your body, the more it awakens. Invite your body deva to retrieve and hold all responsibility for meeting its needs. The more responsible your body deva is for itself, the more empowered it will be.

STAYING IN THE SADDLE

Think of your experience in the human form as similar to riding a horse. Your horse has its own consciousness. Let your body deva acknowledge its own consciousness while you sit in the saddle.

My guides walked me through one other process during my

meditation with my body deva. They instructed me to pull all my energy off my arms and legs and into my divine line — essentially, to get in my saddle. When I did this, I felt a huge rush of energy as my divine line expanded, as well as a flow of joy, freedom, and connection.

As soon as I pulled all my energy into my channel/saddle, my body deva felt the space I had just created, and she filled every aspect of herself with her own essence and light.

The specific request is this: *"I invite my Higher Self to work with my energetic fields and the guides to pull all my energy into my divine line and firmly attach to the front of my spine. I invite my body deva at the level of its Higher Self to infuse every cell, organ, meridian, and gland with the vibration of its essence."*

When you hold your energy in your divine line, you will feel grounded, safe, and supported. Your body deva will feel more supported as the light flows more effortlessly in your own divine lines. This will also positively affect your chakras, which are your energy centers.

Here is another good reason to connect with your body deva. Because your Soul essence and body deva inhabit the same physical body, there is the potential for conflict. If you are unaware of your body deva, the conflicts may not resolve easily. These conflicts may create physical and emotional challenges. You may not be able to commit to a specific diet or exercise regime. Compulsive spending, rebellion, overexertion, insomnia, procrastination, or laziness may also be indicators of conflict between you and your body deva.

If you feel as if you and your body deva are in conflict, you can invite the Higher Selves of you and your body deva to resolve your conflicts in the higher realms. You can ask the Higher Selves of you and your body deva to connect with angelic advisers to help the two of you resolve your differences and develop a healthy, cocreative relationship.

Your body consciousness may be a few steps behind your Soul consciousness. Think of yourself as the gentle, compassionate, patient teacher. Your body deva is the student and is learning from you as you model right energy.

Your body deva also has things it can teach you. It is a master at manifesting, creating, and receiving. When you and your body deva connect in a healthy way, you will learn from each other and create what you each desire.

GIVING RESPONSIBILITY BACK TO YOUR BODY DEVA

Once you recognize your body deva's consciousness, you are ready for the next step: letting go of your body deva's responsibilities. When you give responsibilities back to your body deva, it will move into empowerment and self-control.

Your body deva can be responsible for itself; it can decide what to eat, when to exercise, when to sleep, when to rest, and when to play. It is pulsed by its own desires. Over time, the more the body deva cultivates self-love, self-control, and personal responsibility, the more it will move into healthier habits. If you override your body deva, it will rebel.

For years, I held all the control and the responsibility for my body. At the end of the day, my body's mantra was, "I am going to do whatever I want to do." So my body would eat and drink whatever she wanted and stay up late. I finally realized my body was rebelling against being overly controlled.

When I handed back her responsibilities, she stopped rebelling. She began to feel as if she was in control of herself and became more empowered. After a few months, my body stopped engaging in unhealthy behavior. I was more rested and shed a few pounds. The inner conflict resolved, and we both enjoyed the ride with far less struggle. What a relief!

The best way to address the pattern of overcontrolling your body is to lift all your energetic control nuggets off your body deva and hold them in your own divine line. The vibration of control actually serves as a great energetic glue or Velcro that can help you stay in your divine line and firmly attach to the front of your spine.

The specific protocol is this: *"I invite my Higher Self to work with my energetic fields and the guides to lift all my control off my body deva and to bring it back to my divine line. I ask that all responsibilities belonging to my body deva be returned to its Higher Self."*

You can only control the energy in your own divine line. The more you hold awareness and responsibility for the vibrations in your divine line, the more your body will be responsible for itself. The more it holds responsibility for itself, the more empowered your body will be.

Healing Feelings of Abandonment in Your Body Deva

Every time you have incarnated in this world, the same body deva has hosted you. It changes its form to accommodate your level of consciousness. Each time death occurs, your body deva may experience a sense of separation, which in turn may trigger feelings of abandonment.

I learned about this one morning in meditation when I asked my body deva how she was feeling. She told me she was worried that I would leave this physical plane.

"Yes, one day I will transition back into my light body, which exists in a different realm," I replied.

"And you are going to leave me, like you always do."

"What do you mean, 'Like I always do'?" I was feeling a little clueless.

My body deva answered, "Each time you come to Earth, you ride with me. I am the same nature spirit each lifetime."

I needed a minute to digest what she had just said. Each time I come to Earth, I am assigned the same nature spirit? Really?

She continued, "I remember all the lifetimes you have ever had here because it was me you rode inside. Each lifetime, I change to match the needs of our current evolution. Sometimes I am in male form, sometimes female. My skin color and ancestral lineage change, depending on what you set up for yourself for each incarnation."

When I asked if she evolved in each lifetime as well, she answered, "Yes, a little, but you have never been awake enough to help me in my evolution, so my process of evolution has been much slower compared to yours."

When I asked why, she responded, "Because until now, my process has not been a conscious one."

I was starting to get the point. "So, all this fear of abandonment is more about all the times I died and was not even aware of your unique consciousness?"

"Yes!" she said, sounding very relieved that I was finally getting it.

Wow, was that a surprise. After this discovery, I worked with my body deva to help release and heal all the moments she ever felt abandoned by me. I realized that one of the body deva's core issues is abandonment.

When you help your body deva heal this core issue, it will feel a greater sense of connection, support, safety, and love. And as your body deva shifts, you will also experience greater confidence, support, and empowerment. Here's how to do it.

Helping Your Body Heal Abandonment

Take a few deep breaths into your belly. Bring your awareness into your divine line. Firmly attach your divine line to the front of your spine. Travel up to the level of your Higher Self. Ask your Higher Self to connect with your body deva's Higher Self. Once the connection has been made, make the following request: "*I invite you, body deva, at the level of your Higher Self, to work with your energetic fields and the guides to place healing holograms, sounds, and light around all the moments you ever felt abandoned in all incarnations.*"

Now imagine your body deva spinning orbs of light and healing energy around itself.

Continue by saying, "*I ask that you, body deva, retrieve all responsibilities for connecting and committing to yourself. I invite my Higher Self to work with my energetic fields to return all responsibility for connecting or committing to you, my body deva. I invite you, my body deva, to hold responsibility for yourself and use your unique gifts, wisdom, and mastery to meet those needs in your own divine line and at the level of your Higher Self. I ask that all trauma from all the moments of abandonment be gently dissolved and replaced with the vibration of the spiritual lesson, which is connection and commitment to your own essence and your own evolution.*"

This protocol is a combination of the Fourth and Fifth Cups. You are using the challenge of abandonment to flip it into the solution of connection. When your body deva releases its fear of abandonment and loss, it is ready for the next step. Your body may have forgotten that it is from Earth, that it consists of the earthly elements, such as water, minerals, and air. When your body remembers that it is an expression of Earth, it will experience a greater sense of support. It will also have an easier time creating what it desires.

Increasing Connection to Earth

As I helped my body deva release its fear of abandonment, my guides walked me through another protocol. This process helped my body deva feel a greater sense of connection to Earth, her true mother.

First I was instructed to travel up my divine line and feel my divine spark in the heart of Source. As I traveled up my divine line for what seemed like a very long time, I eventually came to a little spark. This spark was simple and pure. As I held my awareness at the level of my divine spark, my guides asked if I could perceive the divine spark of Earth in Source.

I asked my Higher Self to find the divine spark of Earth. After a few moments, I was able to perceive a much larger spark emitting an exquisite vibration of sweetness.

I invited my body deva at the level of her Higher Self to travel up her divine line to her divine spark. As she did so, she perceived that her spark was a part of the Earth's spark.

My body deva felt a huge wave of connection and support coursing through her spine as she made this connection. Her fears of abandonment, of not having enough, and of not being supported instantly dissolved. She felt a strong and beautiful connection to Earth and the entire nature kingdom.

Perhaps your body deva has forgotten that it really is from Earth, just as you may have forgotten that you are not your body. Here is the protocol to help your body deva remember its connection to Earth.

Remembering the Connection to Earth

"I invite my body deva at the level of its Higher Self to use its energetic fields to extend its divine line, which runs through the spine

into the heart of the Earth, and connect with the divine line of Earth. I invite my body deva to remember that it is an expression of Earth."

Hold space for your body deva to remember its connection. When your body deva feels its connection to the divine line of Earth, it will feel safer and more supported and protected. It will also be able to pull on all the energetic resources for manifesting.

Helping Your Body Heal

In addition to fears of abandonment, your body deva deals with physical health issues. Fortunately, your body deva is designed to heal itself. The only variable is how fast. Can it heal quickly enough to maintain health in every cell and system? Like you, your body deva is energetically sensitive. It can take on issues, responsibilities, and energies that do not belong to it. When it struggles with these issues, it becomes diseased and ages more quickly.

Your body deva is incredibly complex and intelligent. It will do the best it can to maintain health. When you clean up your body's energetic diet, health is often restored. Here's a protocol for helping you do just that.

Helping Your Body Hold a Healthier Vibration

Think of one area in your body that needs healing or balancing. It could be a body part, an organ, a meridian line, or a gland. Pick just one for now.

Silently or out loud speak the specific words of this protocol: *"I invite my body deva at the level of its Higher Self to work with its energetic fields to energetically locate the area that needs healing. I invite my body deva to release all vibrations, responsibilities, issues, and energy that it is holding in this area that do not belong to my body deva. I ask my body deva's Higher Self to place healing shapes, sounds, and vibrations around the (body part, organ, gland, and so on) in a way that heals, repairs, and aligns this area for the greatest level of health and vitality."*

Take a moment to imagine your body deva's Higher Self doing this work in the higher realms. This simple protocol can help your body deva heal. The more you ask your body deva to use its Higher Self, the stronger this energetic aspect of it becomes.

MANIFESTING YOUR DESIRES

Your body deva can also support you in this world, if you let it. Like millions of people, I have watched the movie *The Secret*. I tried the manifestation techniques in it, but nothing happened. I learned the *real* secret from an eleven-year-old girl.

Sarah and I had been working together since she was five. Her level of sensitivity and wisdom always astounded me. Although I saw her only three or four times a year, we were comfortable with each other. Her mother joined us as Sarah climbed up on my water-filled sound table (a massage table filled with water and speakers embedded into the table).

Sarah turned to her mother and said, "Oh, Mom! Please, please, please, can we get one of these beds for my bedroom? I bet I would not have any more anxiety."

"So, you are having anxiety?" I asked, as I placed my hands on her feet and silently called in her guides for her healing session.

"Well, I get really anxious when I want something and I can't get it."

"Well, shall we look at how to help you get what you want in the world?"

I took a few deep breaths and pulled my awareness into my

divine line. I traveled up to my Higher Self and posed the question out loud with my eyes closed. "How can Sarah create what she wants for herself in the physical world?"

I relaxed as some higher aspect of Sarah, the guides, and me gathered the information.

A few seconds later, I saw Sarah's body deva come forward.

I asked, "Sarah, does your body have its own energy that is different from you, or are you the same as your body?"

"It has its own energy. I call her Lola," she said.

I smiled and thought to myself, "This eleven-year-old is so far ahead of me."

Pausing for a moment in humility, I asked, "Can you see her?"

"Yes, I can always see her, silly! I ride inside her."

I had not spoken to Sarah about the body deva consciousness. This concept was something I was still discovering and unpacking.

"Can you ask your body what she likes to do?"

Sarah closed her eyes, scrunched up her face, and moved her lips as she silently conversed with Lola.

After a few moments of silent conversation, Sarah gasped and opened her eyes in surprise. "Lola said that she likes to make stuff. She says her job is to create."

"Sarah, ask Lola if she has been holding the responsibility for creating, or whether that is a job you have been holding for her."

Sarah closed her eyes again, and a few moments later said, "Lola said that I have been holding that job instead of her. So, I just sent it back to her. She is going to get busy getting what she wants for herself." This all poured out of Sarah in a flurry of excitement.

Her mom and I exchanged glances, slightly shocked and amazed.

"So, your body's job is to manifest and create in the physical world?"

"Yeah, that's what she said. It makes sense. She is physical, and I am not."

"This is true. You are just a beam of light, and a beautiful one, I might add," I said, smiling.

Sarah laughed. "I can see my light, and it's really bright. Sometimes I feel like I have to wear sunglasses when I look inside."

"Sarah, if your body is now responsible for creating and manifesting in the physical world, what is your job?"

Sarah grew quiet and closed her eyes. She took a deep breath, and I felt energy starting to swirl within and around her.

I guided Sarah through the next layer. "Sarah, if you hold the energy of what you want, like happiness, inside your river of light, then your body goes and gets things in the outer world that are like the energy of what you are holding inside. Like, if you had this water table in your bedroom, you might feel happy, and safe, and supported. So if you feel that happiness, safety, and support in your river of light/divine line, then your body might be able to create a situation that is the reflection of the energy you are holding inside yourself."

Sarah said, "I understand. I think this is going to be fun. Thanks, Aleya."

I laughed with tears in my eyes and said, "No, thank you, and I thank Lola too."

Over the years, the more Sarah focused on her inner reality, the more her outer reality manifested for her. She did not manifest trivial things like a sound table. But she did help her body cultivate particular qualities in its divine line, such as focus, clarity, empowerment, self-appreciation, and self-love. She got into the schools of her choice and had wonderful boyfriends and a supportive circle of friends. Her increased empowerment and connection to her body deva helped her navigate her adolescence with far greater grace and ease.

The Magic of Manifesting

Imagine the feeling of having your desires fulfilled. Activate that vibration at the level of the Higher Selves of you, your body deva, and your Team. Imagine you, your body deva, and your Team all engaging in this desired manifestation in the higher realms. Invite that reflection to occur in the physical realm. Trust that the work is happening. Trust opens your channels to receive. Be patient. Manifestation does not usually happen overnight, but it can.

Let's Practice Manifesting

Think of something you would like to manifest in your life. If you had that thing or situation in your life, how would you feel? Happy? Safe? Supported? Loved? Pick the strongest need or feeling.

Use this protocol: *"I ask the Higher Selves of me, my body deva, and my Team to activate the vibration of (the feeling you identified) in our divine lines and at the level of our Higher Selves."*

Take a moment for the magic to happen in the higher realms. Imagine you, your body deva, and your Team all activating this quality in your divine lines. Then imagine these desires manifesting in the higher realms. Maybe you wish for a healthy, fit body, a beloved partner, or greater financial stability. Whatever you desire, see it happening in the higher realms. See your body deva using its connections with the entire nature kingdom to manifest this intention in the higher realms. Ask that this higher dimensional reality be reflected into this one.

When you sit in meditation with your body deva, ask it what it wants. Give it permission to manifest its desires. This is a very empowering experience for your body deva. If your body deva is happy, you will be too.

DAILY RITUAL FOR CONNECTING WITH YOUR BODY DEVA

The more you pay attention to your body deva, the stronger the connection becomes. Every day for the next three months, ask your Higher Self to return all responsibilities it is holding for your body deva. Ask that these responsibilities be returned to your body deva at the level of its Higher Self. Invite the Higher Self of your body deva to retrieve all responsibilities for itself that it has given to others (especially parents). Give permission to your body deva to be responsible for its own reality.

Begin a daily ritual of connecting with your body deva nature spirit. When you wake up in the morning, say, "Good morning, body deva."

Ask your body deva what organic, unprocessed foods it wants to eat. Every morning ask your body deva what clothes it wants to wear. Ask your body deva what it wants to do on Sunday. Spend time in nature. It is how your body connects with Earth/itself. Take baths, and invite your body deva to relax. Give your body deva permission to sleep in a few times a month, if possible. Invite your body deva to pick and choose music and aromatherapy as a way of helping it balance its energy. Ask your body deva what kind of regular exercise it wants to get. Get regular massage and/ or acupuncture, or other modalities that can help your body deva stay balanced and healthy.

INSIGHTS AND THINGS TO REMEMBER

- Your body is a nature spirit.
- Your body is from Earth.
- Your body has a consciousness that is different from yours.
- You are a beam of light riding in your body on the front of your spine.

- Your body deva is responsible for meeting all its own needs.
- Your body deva may be a few steps behind you in its evolution.
- You can model energy to your body deva. It will do what you model.
- Treat your body deva with patience and kindness. How would you treat a horse you're riding?

The How

Let's dive into the spiritual lab and practice the quick steps as well as the full protocol for connecting with your body. At the end of the chapter, you can use the audio meditation to help you connect more deeply with your body deva.

The Quick Steps

With your inhale or your imagination, bring your awareness into your divine line. Invite your Higher Self to firmly attach your divine line onto the front of the spine. Travel up your divine line to the level of your Higher Self. Invite your Higher Self to connect with the Higher Self of your body deva nature spirit. Hold an awareness that the connection is happening at the level of your Higher Selves. Invite your body deva at the level of its Higher Self to recognize its unique wise consciousness. Invite your Higher Self to connect with your own inner wisdom and model that to your body deva. Invite your Higher Self to activate the vibration of your essence in your own divine line and model that to your body deva. Invite your body deva at the level of its Higher Self to locate its own divine line and activate the vibration of its essence in its own divine line. Invite the Higher Selves of you and your body deva to create healthy grids of connection between yourselves in the higher realms. Send all responsibilities that either of you may be holding for the other back to their right and perfect place. Hold a gentle awareness, and invite your Higher Self and your body's Higher Self to send appropriate information to each other. Update the reference points for you and your body deva.

THE FULL PROTOCOL

1. Bring your awareness into your divine line. Take a few conscious breaths, and on an inhale, ask your Higher Self to work with your energetic fields to pull all your energy off of everyone and everything and to bring it back to your divine line, which flows on the front of your spine. Speak the following words out loud or silently: *"I invite my Higher Self to work with my energetic fields and the guides to pull all my energy and awareness off of everyone and everything and back to my divine line, which flows on the front of my spine."* Hold awareness that some energetic aspect of you is bringing your awareness back to your divine line. Close your eyes, and imagine standing in your inner river of light.

2. Invite your Higher Self to firmly attach your divine line onto the front of the spine: *"I ask my Higher Self to work with my energetic fields and the guides to firmly attach my divine line to the front of my spine."* Take a breath, and let this energetic aspect of you do this work. Let go and allow. Get spacey. Let your Higher Self do the work. You might feel little swirls of energy within and around you as the work happens. You may even doze off for a moment.

3. Using your imagination, travel up your divine line to the level of your Higher Self. Close your eyes, and imagine standing in your own divine river of light. Imagine traveling up this column of light to the level of your Higher Self.

4. Invite your Higher Self to connect with the Higher Self of your body deva nature spirit: *"I ask my Higher Self to work with my energetic fields and the guides to connect with my body deva's Higher Self."*

5. Hold an awareness that the connection is happening at the level of your Higher Selves.

6. Invite your body deva at the level of its Higher Self to recognize its unique and wise consciousness: *"I invite my body deva at the level of its Higher Self to work with its energetic fields and the guides to recognize its own unique wisdom and consciousness."*

7. Model that same energy to your body deva. At the level of your Higher Self, recognize the unique light and wisdom that flow in your divine line.

8. Invite your Higher Self to activate the vibration of your essence in your divine line and to model that to your body deva: *"I ask my Higher Self to work with my energetic fields and the guides to activate the vibration of my essence in my divine line."*

9. Invite your body deva at the level of its Higher Self to activate the vibration of its essence in its divine line: *"I invite my body deva at the level of its Higher Self to work with its energetic fields and the guides to activate the vibration of its essence in its divine line, which flows through the spine."*

10. Invite the Higher Selves of you and your body deva to create healthy grids of connection between yourselves: *"I invite the Higher Selves of me and my body deva to create healthy open grids of love, connection, balance, empowerment, personal responsibility and clarity between us. I ask the Higher Selves of me and my body deva to activate vibrations of connection, safety, empowerment, and peace in our individual divine lines and to reflect that upon each other."*

11. Send all responsibilities that either of you is holding that are not yours back to their right and perfect place: *"I invite the Higher Selves of me and my body deva to locate all responsibilities that we are individually holding that are not ours, and to return them to their right and perfect place."*

12. Invite your Higher Self and your body deva's Higher Self to send appropriate information to each other: *"I invite my Higher Self and my body deva's Higher Self to send all appropriate information to each other in the higher realms."*

13. Hold awareness that in this higher realm you and your body deva are having an energetic conversation. Imagine your body deva holding responsibility for loving, supporting, protecting, honoring, and recognizing itself. Imagine the energetic aspect of you in this higher realm doing the same.

14. Update all reference points: *"I ask that all reference points are updated for me and my body deva."*

15. Take a breath and relax. Do a little inner assessment. How do you feel? How does your body feel?

FIFTH CUP AUDIO MEDITATION

To listen to the audio meditation for the Fifth Cup, go to www.cupsofconsciousness.com/meditations.

Increasing Connection and Empowerment in the Body Deva

This meditation empowers your body deva by helping it connect with its own essence and hold appropriate responsibility.

May you and your body deva model healthy energy to each other, and may you both enjoy the ride!

6 SIXTH CUP

Your Soul Has Wisdom and Inner Gifts

Embrace and use your wisdom and your gifts.

*T*he old adage "Give someone a fish, and you feed him for a day; teach someone to fish, and you feed him for a lifetime" speaks to the Sixth Cup. Use your wisdom for yourself, and create a life of abundance.

Your Soul has spent many incarnations cultivating wisdom and is intent on gaining more wisdom in this lifetime. I think of your Soul's wisdom as your inner gifts. This wisdom creates a vibration that flows like a current in your divine line. When you tap into your wisdom, you access higher consciousness. The Sixth Cup is all about how to do this.

There are four aspects to this cup. First, learn to identify your gifts. Second, learn how to use your gifts. Third, discover how to cultivate new gifts. Finally, learn how to avoid the challenges that can come with your gifts. As you strengthen your inner gifts, you increase your capacity to be supported and to help others in a healthy manner.

Identify Your Soul's Gifts

What qualities do you and others value about you? Are you kind? Patient? Trustworthy? Supportive? Funny? Positive? Discerning? Respectful? Identify one positive adjective you would use to describe yourself.

Take a deep breath, pull yourself into your divine line, and imagine this quality flowing like a stream of light in your divine line. The more you focus on the vibration, the more the flow will grow.

Explore this vibration. Recognize how it supports, protects, and sustains you. Increase your appreciation of the inner wisdom. After all, you have spent lifetimes cultivating it.

As you develop a deeper awareness of your inner wisdom, your sense of self-worth will increase. Here is a protocol to help you identify, activate, and amplify your Soul gifts.

Locating the Gifts

"I invite the Higher Selves of me, my body deva, and my Team to work with the energetic fields and the guides to locate, activate, and amplify the vibration of our Souls' wisdom at the level of our Higher Selves and in our individual divine lines."

Let the energetic aspects of you, your body deva, and your Team do the work in the higher realms and activate the vibration of your wisdom in your divine lines. Over time, your wisdom will reflect into your energy fields and conscious awareness. You may be feeling it already.

When you, your body deva, and your Team all hold your particular pearls of wisdom and inner gifts in your own divine lines, you will experience an abundant and amazing reflection in your physical life.

Use Your Inner Gifts

The second aspect of the Sixth Cup is using your unique gifts. These gifts can serve as your primary support mechanism; the more you use your gifts, the more you will be supported in the world.

I learned this one day while sitting on the beach in Santa Barbara, waiting for my phone to ring, and thinking about how to grow my private practice. Starting a new practice in a town where I only knew a handful of people was proving to be more difficult than I had anticipated, plus my low bank account balance was weighing me down.

Taking a deep breath, I pulled all my awareness off my bank account and brought it into my divine line. I felt my guides encircle me. I asked, "How can I increase financial support in my life?"

I felt wise words drifting in from above. My guides shared the following protocol to help me retrieve all responsibility for supporting myself as well as for increasing the vibration of my Soul's inner gift. I used this protocol daily, and within a few weeks, my phone started ringing and my practice bloomed.

If you feel the need for greater support in your life, financially, physically, spiritually, or in relationships, use this protocol. It will help you hold responsibility for supporting yourself. You will also become more deeply aware that your support comes from your inner wisdom and gifts, not from the outer world.

INCREASING SUPPORT

Pull all your awareness into your divine line, and firmly attach to the front of your spine. Holding your awareness in your divine line or traveling up to your Higher Self, make the following request: *"I invite my Higher Self to work with my energetic fields and the guides to retrieve all responsibility for being supported and to hold that responsibility at the level of my Higher Self. I ask that all my reference points for support be lifted off of everyone and everything and brought back to my divine line. I ask that the vibration of my Soul's inner gift, greatest wisdom, and mastery be activated, at the level of my Higher Self and in my divine line. I ask that these inner gifts that flow in my divine line be my primary source of support. I ask that all my reference points for support be updated."*

Use your imagination, and hold your awareness in your divine line or at the level of your Higher Self. Imagine your Higher Self activating this vibration. You do not need to consciously know what your inner gifts, wisdom, and mastery are at first. As your Higher Self activates this vibration, you will begin to feel it, and then your mind will know.

Imagine your Higher Self retrieving all responsibility as well as your energetic reference points for support. You might even give your Higher Self a cosmic vacuum cleaner to pull all your responsibilities and reference points for support back to your divine line.

Imagine or feel a stream of support flowing in your divine line instead of on money, people, or things. The more you reference your support in direct connection with the vibration and flow of your inner gifts and wisdom in your divine line, the more you will be supported in the world.

When I did this protocol for the first time, I felt comforted. It was as if a pure, crystal stream of light was flowing within me. I realized that one of my gifts was clarity. As I acknowledged this inner gift, I was received and appreciated to a greater degree in my outer world.

Using Your Gifts for Support

The more you hold your inner gifts in yourself, the more support you will feel. If you are attached to other people's behavior or journeys, you may be energetically placing your gifts on them.

Over many years I have successfully cultivated the vibration of peace in my divine line. If I try to make others peaceful by projecting my gift onto them, my inner peace will decrease. The healthier way to create peace is to hold the vibration of peace in myself. The next step is to give myself permission to desire and be responsible for only my own inner peace, not that of others. As I hold my inner peace, I create a positive empathic field. Those around me will empathically feel my inner peace and begin to activate the vibration of peace for themselves in their own way.

This healthy stance is the following: *"I am responsible for receiving my own gifts, wisdom, and mastery. I am supported by my inner gifts, and I will model that in the world."* Invite the Higher Selves of you, your body deva, and your Team to hold this stance in all realms where you express yourselves.

Your inner gifts, such as self-love, inner peace, and self-respect, are qualities that not only support you but also draw to you beautiful situations and create healthy relationships.

After sipping on the Sixth Cup for several years, I began to realize the power of this concept during an energy healing session with one of my clients. Susan reached for the tissue box and said,

"Aleya, I am so freaked out right now. If I don't sell my house in the next month, I'll lose it to foreclosure."

Susan got on the table. I draped a silk scarf over her feet, took a deep breath, and pulled myself into my divine line. I called in the Ascended Masters and Susan's guides, traveled up to my Higher Self, and asked, "Susan, at the level of your Higher Self, why did you create this situation regarding your home and finances?"

Susan's Higher Self slowly digested the question. Then, in the quietest voice, in the higher realms, I heard her Higher Self respond, "I use all my energy to support others."

"Susan, do you feel as if you're always supporting other people?" I asked out loud.

"Absolutely! I have done that since I was a little girl. All I wanted was for others to feel the incredible flow of support that I felt inside myself as a child. I remember on my tenth birthday, my dad came home from work, and after dinner he told us that he had been fired that day. We had to sell our house and move back to his parents' home, six hours away. I had to change schools and friends. I was devastated. I thought if I used all my inner support to help my Dad, it would somehow magically make life better. I learned the hard way that it didn't. Right at that time in my life I stopped feeling that magical inner support. I wish I could get that inner support back."

"Let me see if I can help you. It looks like you need that right about now."

She nodded as the tears started to slowly trickle down her cheeks.

I closed my eyes. "Susan, at the level of your Higher Self, would you be willing to use all your gifts, resources, wisdom, and energy of support on yourself?"

"That would be selfish," her Higher Self immediately responded.

"What if you held all your gifts on yourself and modeled that to others, which in turn would help others learn how to support themselves?" I asked.

When Susan's Higher Self said that she didn't know how, I offered to show her. "Susan, at the level of your Higher Self, using your energetic fields and the guides, locate all the spiritual gifts, wisdom, and mastery of support that you have placed on others in all incarnations. Bring these vibrations of support back to your Higher Self. I invite your Team members and your body deva to do the same at the level of their Higher Selves."

I saw her Higher Self using a magical butterfly net. She was swooping it down and lifting beautiful bundles of light off of others and bringing them back to herself.

"I invite you to clean, clear, and realign your gifts, wisdom, and mastery of support for yourself."

Susan's Higher Self brought out a silk scarf and polished her gifts. She then reembedded them into her divine line.

"At the level of your Higher Self, send the appropriate energetic information to everyone you were trying to support."

A few moments later, I saw her Higher Self emitting beams of light with energetic information in hundreds of different directions. I silently invited her body deva, at the level of its Higher Self, and her Team members to do the same. It was like watching a flurry of energetic emails being sent into hyperspace.

I continued, "I invite you to lift your desire for everyone to be supported off of others and to bring it back to you. I invite you to return all responsibilities for supporting others to their Higher Selves, along with all relevant and appropriate information. Release all empathic sensitivity around issues of support that are not yours, as well as any karma that does not belong to you."

Susan took a deep breath, and the tears started again. "Aleya, I feel a huge weight lifting off me right now. My mind does not understand it, but I somehow feel free and so incredibly light."

I asked if we could work a bit longer, and she agreed. "I invite you, Susan, at the level of your Higher Self, to work with your energetic fields and the guides to activate your spiritual gifts and your vibrations of support at the level of your Higher Self and in your divine line."

I could see little sparkles beginning to light up within and around her. The energy began to swirl, and a deep current of support started to flow in her divine line.

"Susan, you are a master of support. The good thing is that you have spent lifetimes cultivating this energy of support inside yourself. It is something you never lose. It is designed only for you, no one else. If you hold it in yourself and model it to others, you will help people in a more empowered way, and you will benefit as well from your inner gift," I said.

Susan asked, "How can I keep this amazing feeling I have right now?"

When I instructed her to take a deep breath and use each inhale to pull herself into her divine line, Susan took a few deep, conscious breaths.

"I invite your Higher Self to work with your energetic fields to pull all your awareness and energy into your divine line."

"I am in," she said.

"Travel up your divine line to your Higher Self."

A few moments later, her energy fields expanded. "I am there," she said.

"Ask your Higher Self to activate your mastery of support at the level of your Higher Self and in your divine line."

Her lips moved and her eyelids fluttered as she made her silent request.

"Stay in your divine line, and just watch your Higher Self do the work," I instructed.

"I can feel it happening!" she exclaimed.

"Can you feel yourself holding your mastery of support for yourself and not for others?" I asked.

"Yes. I never realized this before, but this vibration of support is complex. I can feel how it is designed only for me. In fact, if I put it on someone else, I think it might actually weigh someone down, as opposed to helping," she said.

"Yes, exactly. The moment you place your gift on another, you are less able to use it for yourself. This gift is designed for you, no one else. Every time you want to support another person, bring your awareness into your divine line and then up to the level of your Higher Self.

"Ask your Higher Self to activate the vibration of support at the level of your Higher Self and in your divine line. Invite your Higher Self to send all the energetic information you have regarding support to the person you want to help. Invite that person to receive it where he or she can and to the degree he or she chooses. Then make sure you are holding all your desire for supporting yourself on yourself and not on the other person. Return any responsibility you might be holding for supporting this person. Then model the solution of what you want for this person in yourself."

Susan said, "I think I get it."

"Imagine hitting a save button inside yourself so that you can instantly come back to this vibration and energetic stance whenever you wish."

As she hit her inner save button, I quietly said, "This is your mastery. You never lose it. The only question is: *Are you going to use it on yourself?*"

She nodded her head and said, "In every breath."

As Susan sat down, she looked down at her phone and saw a text come through. "Oh, my God! You will not believe this! Well, maybe you will," she said, laughing. "I just got a text from my Realtor saying that the people who put a lowball offer on my house last month have come back and are offering my asking price. They want to close in thirty days."

Susan successfully sold her house within the month. Changes in the physical dimension do not usually happen ten minutes after an inner shift, but on that day they did.

Susan continued her sessions with me for several years. I helped her focus on holding her inner support on herself instead of on others. After six months, she received a job promotion and met an amazing man. Two years later, they married and bought a beautiful home in the Santa Barbara foothills.

The exterior was far less important to her than it had been before. What really mattered was the comfort Susan received when she held her inner support inside herself. In addition, Susan's fear of loss evaporated as she realized that she would always be supported in the outer world as long as she felt the support internally. She still had rough days, but she now had an empowered supportive baseline.

If you are struggling, see if you have placed your gifts externally. Are you holding and using them for yourself? Or are you using them on others? If you are trying to change another person's life for the better, how are you doing that? Are you modeling the solution to her and sending her energetic information that can help her empower herself?

Appreciate and use the qualities you have cultivated inside yourself. You will have a more positive and more powerful impact on others.

CULTIVATE YOUR GIFTS

The third aspect of this cup is cultivating your Soul's gifts. As you evolve, the qualities you value change. A highly conscious being may value compassion, whereas someone else may value power.

Your spiritual journey informs you about what qualities you want to cultivate. As you grow, you will feel the urge to develop new, more complex inner gifts. Knowing how to do this can be very useful.

When I met my husband, I was in awe of his discipline. Whatever he set his heart and mind to do, he accomplished. I realized that his gift of discipline afforded him a level of freedom and power. I wanted that too, so I pulled out my magic wand, and poof, I wrote this book in forty days! Just kidding. It took me a bit longer than forty days to write this book. But after several years I have successfully attained a certain amount of discipline.

Use the following protocol to help you cultivate the qualities you desire.

WHAT QUALITIES DO YOU WANT TO EMBODY?

Think of a quality you would like to embody. Do you desire empowerment, self-control, self-love, grace, kindness, patience, trust, discernment, clarity, peace, inner connection? These are just a few suggestions. Whatever the quality may be, hold it in your conscious awareness.

Then say, *"I invite the Higher Selves of me, my body deva, and my Team to work with our energetic fields and the guides to activate the vibration, thought forms, emotions, consciousness, and behaviors of (the quality you desire) at the level of our Higher Selves and in our divine lines."*

Imagine the Higher Selves of you, your body deva, and your Team members embodying this quality in the higher realms. Cultivate the qualities you value, as opposed to the qualities you think you "should" have. The people in your life may project onto you what they think you should embody. Certainly you may take their opinions into consideration, but listen more closely to your own heart's desires.

Use this protocol once a week or every time you think about attaining this quality. The more you do it, the stronger it will become.

Another aspect that the Sixth Cup teaches us to cultivate is safety. You can use the vibrations that flow in your divine line as a safety protection mechanism. After all, *the safest place to be is in your divine line.*

When you look for and find an inner current of safety flowing in your divine line, you will create safe situations. I learned this one evening while walking on the beach.

The sun had just set, and I was hankering for a beach walk. As I got out of my car and headed down the steps to the beach, I saw a man in black sweats leaning up against his car, watching me. He followed me down the beach. I could feel my body deva's hackles go up. Fear started to flow. I could turn around, but then I would have to cross paths with him. No one else was on the beach, a sheer cliff was to my right, and water was to my left. I could spontaneously sprout a mermaid tail and swim off, or I could activate the vibration of safety in the divine line of me, my body deva, and my Team. The latter seemed a bit easier in that moment.

As soon as I activated that vibration, my fear receded. I continued walking, and within a few minutes, the man stopped following me, turned around, and disappeared. It might have been a coincidence, but I consistently practice this technique any time I feel in danger, especially when flying in little planes or on the LA freeway. My fear always disappears, and my environment continues to reflect my inner safety.

You still need to be discerning and take precautions as you navigate the physical realm, but this can help you cultivate safer environments for yourself. I have used this same technique when I encounter dark energies in other dimensions as well.

The basic principle here is to hold the vibration of safety in your divine line. You do this consciously by asking your Higher Self to activate the vibration of safety at the level of your Higher Self and in your divine line, using your energetic fields. Ask your body deva and your Team members to do the same.

Here is a protocol that can help you increase your sense of safety and protection.

INCREASING SAFETY AND PROTECTION

"I invite the Higher Selves of me, my body deva, and my Team to work with the energetic fields and the guides to retrieve all responsibility for being protected. I ask that we retrieve and hold all our reference points for protection and safety in our own divine lines. We ask that the vibration of safety be activated in our divine lines and at the level of our Higher Selves."

Take a deep breath, and hold your awareness in your divine line. Explore how it feels to have an inner current of safety flowing within you. Pull yourself deeper into your inner river of light, and hold the awareness that you are safe in your divine line. As you embrace that energy, you will feel and be safer.

AVOID THE COMMON CHALLENGES OF SPIRITUAL GIFTS

The fourth and final aspect of the Sixth Cup is learning to avoid the challenges that come with your gifts. If you are not careful, you can drop into spiritual arrogance: the belief that you are better than others because of your beliefs, accomplishments, or lifestyle.

Spiritual arrogance can arise at any time. You can see it in any organized religion, in cults, in a yoga class, or in a drumming circle. There are three types of spiritual arrogance: thinking that you are better than others, asking others to value your values, and being attached to other people's journeys and using your gifts on them, as discussed above.

The first type of arrogance arises when you come to believe that you are gifted, while others are not. You feel your gifts make you special, allowing you to treat everyone else as inferior. The symptoms almost always include judgment and criticism of others. They are not as pure. They don't walk their talk. They don't follow a sugar-, meat-, caffeine-, and alcohol-free diet. They are not organic, vegetarian, green, socially just, environmentally sensitive, or Gaia-centric beings. You might even think, "I am better than they are because they are not as evolved as I am." Whenever you think, "They are not...," check in on your spiritual arrogance. As soon as you increase your appreciation for your own beliefs and take responsibility for your own behaviors (and no one else's), your arrogance will recede. Also hold a compassionate stance for others to engage in the energy they need for their own evolution.

The second type of spiritual arrogance arises when you want others to value the same gifts that you value. You might want people to be as respectful as you are, to act with integrity, or to be compassionate. You are imposing your values on others and judging them as inferior if they do not model your values in your way. When you honor your own values as opposed to projecting them onto another, you will walk a humbler path.

The third type of arrogance is a little more layered. There are times when you might become attached to another person's behavior. For example, you might want someone to act with integrity. This attachment triggers the energetic phenomenon of taking responsibility for another. As you hold this responsibility, you will energetically try to use your gifts, tools, and wisdom on him. If his behavior changes, you may take the credit for his shift, and your arrogance will bloom. If the behavior does not change, you become frustrated that your tools are not working. This can trigger two responses. One reaction may be thinking that there is something wrong with this person and that he is unworthy of your gifts. The other may be feeling that there is something wrong with you and that you are a failure because you could not shift the other person.

The way to end this cycle is to lift your attachments off of everyone. Be attached only to your own behavior. This is also a great solution if you find yourself trying to control others. When you have lifted all attachments off of everyone, ask that all responsibilities you are holding for others be returned to them. Hold responsibility for your own behavior. As always, use your Higher Self, not your mind, to do the work. Model the solution, and hold a compassionate space for others.

I learned about this cycle of arrogance one evening…

Descending Mount Judgment

I felt profound inner peace and love right after my enlightenment experience. Nothing could shake it…except watching the news. One Friday night I swung by a friend's house to say hi. As I walked in the door, I saw that her television was tuned to the news channel. I was instantly mesmerized. Reports of war, rape, and environmental destruction flashed before my eyes. Within two minutes, my peaceful reality had been destroyed by a talking head and horrendous graphic images.

I could feel a deep anger boiling up inside me. Under the anger, I could feel my judgment surface like a fire-breathing dragon. I walked outside and took a few deep breaths.

I watched my emotions and thoughts: *How dare people treat*

Earth with such disrespect? Why are those people in the Middle East still at war? What's wrong with them? I can't believe how cruel people are to each other. Everyone is so unconscious and stupid.

It took only two minutes of the evening news for me to summit Mount Judgment. As I stood at the top of the mountain, my heart closed, and my arrogance rose. My inner light flickered down to a meager flame.

As I felt this drop in consciousness, my guides swirled around me. I closed my eyes, brought my awareness back to my divine line, and focused on my inner flow of light. As soon as my mind was quiet, I heard the wise words coming in from the higher realms.

"Aleya, can you feel how you are desiring others to be in a place of peace, respect, and love?"

"Yes, absolutely," I responded, not being able to imagine why that would not be a good thing. "Everyone should be in a state of inner peace, respect, and love. Right?" I asked indignantly.

"What if others are at a different point in their evolution, and they value control, power, or safety over peace and love?" the guides gently and oh-so-wisely asked.

"I never thought about it like that. I would think everyone would want to be in a state of peace, respect, and love," I responded.

"Maybe they do, but perhaps they do not know how. If you judge them and hold anger in your heart, how is that helping them?"

"It's not," I said, as my energetic tail slowly dropped between my legs.

"What if you held peace, respect, and love in your own heart and modeled that to them? Would that feel better than what you're doing now?"

"Yes. But how do I do that, and will that really help?" I asked.

"Each Soul creates a ripple in the world. The vibrations you hold inside yourself ripple out. If the ripples are strong enough, they will affect others. You have to hold all your attachment, desire, and responsibility for the qualities you hold deep inside yourself. The moment you become attached to someone else's energy or behavior, you drop your coherent field of transformation from one hundred percent to zero."

I asked the guides to walk me through the process.

"Take a deep breath," they instructed. "As you hold all your awareness in your divine line, invite your Higher Self to activate the vibration of peace, self-respect, and love at the level of your Higher Self and in your divine line."

Within a few seconds I could feel my energy start to shift and my heart open.

My guides asked, "Can you feel all the attachment and desire you have placed on others for holding a peaceful, respectful, and loving stance?"

As they asked this question, I saw many cords extending out onto others. At the end of each cord, I saw a little ball of energy.

Reading my energetic process, my guides continued, "Those balls of energy are yours. Lift them off, using your Higher Self and energetic fields. Bring them back to you at the level of your Higher Self. Clean them, clear them, and align them just for you. Only be attached to your own state of peace, respect, and love. That is the only way to create a strong, coherent field of transformation."

I invited my Higher Self to do the work. I felt my Higher Self move into action, a level of peace returned, and I gracefully descended Mount Judgment.

Waves of judgment or arrogance may arise as you climb the ladder of consciousness. As you evolve, you will want to cultivate an even more loving, compassionate stance with others. If you don't, you may remedy your arrogance by creating situations in which you are humbled in some way. Instead of getting pummeled, use your Higher Self to cultivate compassion. It is far easier. Anytime you feel a wave of arrogance, you can use the following protocol.

CLEARING ARROGANCE AND JUDGMENT

Begin by saying, *"I invite the Higher Selves of me, my body deva, and my Team to use our energetic fields and the guides to lift all our attachments and desires for other people's reality and behavior off of them and back to ourselves. I ask that we return all responsibilities that we are holding for others. I ask that we lift all our gifts off of others. I ask that we all hold compassion for others as we model our wisdom, mastery, and gifts and the solution within ourselves. I ask that we send all appropriate information to them at the level of their Higher Selves, where they have the capacity to receive it."*

Imagine the energetic aspects of you, your body deva, and your Team members doing each one of these steps in the higher realms. Give yourself permission to attach to your internal reality. Appreciate how much you have worked to attain the positive qualities inside yourself. The only person who needs to value your gifts is you.

INSIGHTS AND THINGS TO REMEMBER

- The Sixth Cup can help you increase your inner resources and move you into a powerful, healthy, cocreative way of serving.
- Using your gifts on yourself prevents spiritual arrogance and judgment.
- You will experience greater protection and support when you feel the vibrations of your inner gifts in your divine line.

- When you receive your own gifts, others will be more open to receiving and appreciating your gifts more deeply.
- Receiving your gifts helps you cultivate empowerment, humility, and compassion.
- Only desire and be responsible for your own behavior.
- Belief systems, values, and behavior change as your consciousness evolves.

The How

Let's dive into the spiritual lab and practice the quick and full protocols for the Sixth Cup. As always, in the full protocol you can speak the parts in italics either silently or out loud — whatever feels best for you.

The Quick Steps

Hold your awareness in your divine line. Lift all your gifts off of everyone and bring them back to yourselves. Locate and activate the vibration of the inner gifts of you, your body deva, and your Team in your divine lines. Feel that flow in your divine line. Receive, embrace, and appreciate this inner quality you have cultivated. Invite your body deva and Team to hold their awareness in their own divine lines and to appreciate the vibrations of their inner gifts as well.

The Full Protocol

1. Use your conscious breath to pull yourself into your divine line. Invite your Higher Self to work with your energetic fields and guides to lift all your awareness and reference points off of everything and everyone and bring

them back to your divine line. Take a moment, and allow your Higher Self to do the work. Imagine and feel light flowing in a column that runs up and down the front of your spine.

2. Invite your Higher Self to locate and activate the vibration of your Soul's gifts: *"I invite my Higher Self to locate and activate the vibrations of my Soul's gifts, wisdom, and mastery."* Take a moment, and hold awareness that your Higher Self is doing this in the higher realms.

3. Invite your body deva to locate the spiritual gifts it has cultivated for itself: *"I invite my body deva at the level of its Higher Self to work with its energetic fields and guides to locate and activate the vibrations of its gifts, wisdom, and mastery."*

4. Invite your Team members to do the same: *"I invite my Team members at the level of their Higher Selves to work with their energetic fields and the guides to locate and activate the vibrations of their gifts, wisdom, and mastery."*

5. Retrieve all spiritual gifts, wisdom, and mastery that you have placed on others: *"I ask the Higher Selves of me, my body deva, and my Team to retrieve, clean, and recalibrate all spiritual gifts, wisdom, and mastery that we have given to others from all incarnations."* Take a moment to imagine and allow the energetic aspect of you, your body deva, and your Team to retrieve these energetic resources. Imagine cleaning and calibrating them just for yourselves. Explore the intricate and exquisite vibration of your Soul's gifts. You have spent lifetimes designing and creating these particular vibrations specifically for yourself. Invite your body deva and your Team to do the same.

6. Embrace the vibration of your Soul's wisdom and mastery: *"I ask my Higher Self to activate the vibration of my Soul's wisdom and mastery in my divine line."* Imagine and allow the vibration to flow in your divine line. Let go of what that actually looks like in the physical realm. Over time you will begin to feel the vibration. Eventually your mind will know the vibration of your inner gifts, which are your pearls of wisdom.

7. Update all your reference points. Reset your fuel gauge: *"I ask that all the reference points for me, my body deva, and my Team be updated."*

SIXTH CUP AUDIO MEDITATION

To listen to the audio meditation for the Sixth Cup, go to www.cupsofconsciousness.com/meditations.

Receiving Your Soul's Gifts

This meditation can help you locate and retrieve all your Soul's gifts. Use your gifts on yourself, and increase inner support and abundance.

When you use your Soul gifts and model
that vibration in the world, you move into greater service.
As you serve humanity in this way, you become
more abundant and access a higher consciousness.

7 SEVENTH CUP

You Are Perfect

> **Your essence is the light that flows
> in your divine line, and it is perfect and whole.**

*Y*ou are perfect.

Fully experiencing this perfection is a key component of your spiritual journey. When you experience your perfection at a conscious, awakened level, you will be able to easily rise above life's challenges.

During my enlightenment experience, I was acutely aware that I was a beam of light expressing myself from the heart of Source. I was divine perfection. The light that flows within you is also exquisitely beautiful and perfect. The more you hold your awareness in your divine line, the better life keeps getting.

There are three steps to the Seventh Cup. The first is learning to connect with your essence. The second is learning to hold responsibility for connecting and loving your essence. And the third is learning to let go of issues that are not yours and that prevent you from connecting with your essence. As you master these three steps, you will live in a state of divine connection and be conscious of your inner perfection.

Connecting with your essence is natural; you do it all the time. All you need to do is take a breath. Each time you inhale, you move into a deeper level of connection with your essence. Most people forget to breathe deeply or consciously. They connect with their essence but only at a tiny fraction of what is possible. When you breathe consciously, you accelerate your connection with your divine essence. Think of your breath as a type of exercise equipment to help you increase your divine connection. The more you use your breath to consciously pull yourself into your divine line, the more connected you will feel, and the brighter your light will shine.

USING YOUR BREATH TO CONNECT WITH YOUR ESSENCE

Take a deep breath. As you inhale, imagine pulling yourself into your divine line on the front of your spine. Ask your Higher Self to pull all your awareness into your divine line and to activate the vibration, sound, and light of your essence in your divine line. Ask your body deva and your Team, at the level of their Higher Selves, to pull all their awareness into their divine lines and to activate the vibration, sound, and light of their essence in their own divine lines.

Wait. Imagine that the energy selves of you, your body deva, and your Team are doing the work in the higher realms.

Take another deep breath, and as you exhale, imagine standing in the middle of a stream of beautiful light. Each time you inhale, intend for your breath and your Higher Self to pull you deeper into your river of light. In this river you are safe, connected, soothed, and perfect. Breathe in again, and repeat the process. Notice if the connection to your essence gets stronger. In the beginning, do this conscious breathing for five cycles. (Be careful not to hyperventilate.) This is a simple, gentle practice that requires some repetition. When your mind wanders, and you lose your awareness of your divine connection, take a break and come back to it later.

If you do not feel the vibration of your essence flowing within you, just imagine it. Ask your Higher Self to do the work up high. Over time, you will feel the ripple effect as your Higher Self pulls all your awareness into your divine line and activates the vibration of your essence.

The Seventh Cup helps you deeply know that you are a beautiful beam of light. When you love that light, everything else starts to flow. It also helps you feel the state of oneness. When you hold your awareness in your divine line, you are one with everything and act from a place of love.

A conscious breath increases your perception of your divine connection. It strengthens your alignment with your spiritual power, wisdom, and mastery. Just ten conscious breaths a day will increase your consciousness perception of your perfection. So start now, take a deep breath, pull yourself into your divine line, and feel where you are perfect, safe, and whole...

TAKING RESPONSIBILITY FOR CONNECTING WITH YOUR ESSENCE

You alone are responsible for connecting and loving your essence. When you take responsibility for connecting with and loving yourself, you start, well, loving yourself. If you don't take responsibility for doing something, you won't do it.

Have you ever expected someone else's love to be enough? What happened when your mother, father, partner, or friend did not show up for you? Did you feel betrayed? Rejected? Unloved? Abandoned? If so, you gave responsibility for being loved to that person. There is no way anyone other than you can love you to the degree that you desire. *You* are responsible for loving your essence.

The more you love your essence, the more love will be reflected back to you by others. (Remember the Third Cup?) This became very clear to me in a session some years ago.

My client, Jane, was going through a messy divorce with a verbally abusive husband. Her self-love and self-confidence were shattered.

"Aleya, I don't feel any love for myself. For years, I wanted my husband to love me, but it was never enough." The tears started to flow. She went on, "I thought that if I was a good enough mother, kept a clean house, made dinner, and was essentially a super mom and wife that Bruce would love me. How wrong I was."

"Before meeting Bruce, do you remember feeling self-love?" I asked.

She paused and then shook her head. "I was really young, and I always had a boyfriend. I have never been single. Well, not since I was fifteen. Come to think of it, I always wanted my boyfriends and then my husband to be the ones to love me. I never even thought about me loving me, until I started seeing you."

"What about your dad? Did you feel love from him?" I asked.

"Never. Well, that's not entirely true. If I excelled at something, I felt like he loved me, or maybe that was just approval. Most of the time nothing I did was good enough for him."

We talked for another fifteen minutes, unpacking her challenges, until I felt the energy shift. "Is there anything else you want to share with me before you get on the table?" I asked.

"No. I am ready for whatever comes," Jane said.

As Jane settled onto the table, I pulled my awareness deeply into my divine line, anchored my divine line to the front of my spine, and traveled up to my Higher Self. I asked my Higher Self to connect with Jane's Higher Self. As I felt that line of connection open, I scanned all the energy within and around her. I silently asked to see what she truly needed at this time. A few seconds later I heard the word *self-love*.

"Jane, I am connecting with your Higher Self. I am asking what you need right now. Your Higher Self just said, 'Self-love.' Does that resonate?"

"Yes, but if I knew how to do that, I would have done it by now," she said, frustrated.

When I offered to show her how, she agreed, somewhat doubtfully.

"Take a deep breath in, and close your eyes. As you inhale, imagine pulling yourself into a column or tube of light that flows inside you on the front of your spine." As I instructed her, I could feel her energy shift into a more connected, fluid vibration.

As Jane nodded her head, I continued. "Hold your awareness in this light while I work with your Higher Self." Another nod.

"I invite your Higher Self to work with your energetic fields and the guides to activate the vibration, sound, and light of your essence in your divine line at the level of your Higher Self."

I waited and watched her energy self do the work. The guides came closer and said to me, "Model that same energy to Jane right now inside yourself."

I took a deep breath in and silently asked my Higher Self to do the same. As I held my awareness in my divine line, I opened to receive the sound, vibration, and light of my essence. I increased my appreciation and love for my own inner light. As I did this, I felt the light in my divine line amplify. As I modeled that stance to Jane, I felt an increase in her light. My guides said, "Remember the responsibility part."

"Are you ready for the next step, Jane?" I asked.

"Yes, but I can't believe how in just a few minutes I feel so different. My eyes are closed, but all I can see is light. I normally just see darkness. I can actually see and feel a light inside me. I never knew it was there before. What is it?"

"This light is your essence. It's who you truly are," I replied.

Between tears of relief and surprise she said, "But it's so beautiful and sweet."

I handed her some tissue. "I know. That's you. You are just a beautiful beam of light, and that is the only energy you need to love and embrace."

She laughed and said, "Well, that is going to be a whole lot easier. Why didn't I learn this in kindergarten? Okay, I'm ready for the next step."

"Jane, can you imagine what it would feel like if you gave other people responsibility for loving you? At an energetic level that's what you were doing. Instead I am going to invite you to hold responsibility for loving yourself."

I began, "I invite your Higher Self to work with your energetic fields and the guides to retrieve all responsibilities for loving, appreciating, and embracing your essence off of everyone and everything, especially your dad, all past boyfriends, and Bruce." I paused and waited for her Higher Self to move into action. With my eyes closed, I scanned her fields and saw the energetic aspect of her slowly retrieving all responsibilities for loving herself.

"Oh, my God, that feels so much better. I feel so much stronger and not so needy. It's like I am in love with me," she giggled.

I did another energetic scan up high and felt a deep sense of fullness inside her. I asked the guides if there was anything else, and they responded with one word: *perfection.*

"Jane, at the level of your Higher Self, I invite you to lift all your reference points for your perfection and your self-worth off of everyone and everything. Bring them back to you at the level of your Higher Self. I invite you to hold these reference points for your perfection in direct correlation with the light of your essence, which flows in your divine line."

As I completed the protocol, I asked, "Can you imagine looking for your perfection in your divine line instead of in your accomplishments or what others think of you?"

Jane said she thought she could. Then, musing, she added, "I know we didn't talk about Bruce and the divorce, but now when I think about him I don't feel any fear, anger, or grief. How is that possible?"

"When you're meeting your own needs for loving yourself instead of looking for that need to be met by another, you hold greater power, self-confidence, and self-love, and the actions of others matter less."

Remember the Fourth Cup? You do the opposite of what you intend, until you reach a certain level of awareness and you begin to practice what you wish to master.

Jane had collected enough moments of feeling unloved to reach her tipping point. She was ready to flip into self-love, the solution. I congratulated her for being so courageous and so determined to master self-love.

Imagine taking full responsibility for connecting to and loving the divine light that flows within you. Use your Higher Self and your energy fields to help you retrieve all the responsibility to love you that you may have given to others. You might also be holding responsibility for loving others. When you return this responsibility, you will move into a healthy, cocreative relationship with those you love.

The best way to understand this cup is to feel it. Take a

moment now to hold responsibility for connecting with your essence. Remember to read each step of the protocol and then to wait. Give yourself permission to be spacey and to feel the work in the higher realms, as opposed to in your mind.

CONNECTING WITH YOUR ESSENCE

1. Close your eyes, and take five deep breaths. Pull your awareness into your divine line, and firmly attach your divine line to the front of your spine. Make the following requests silently or out loud:

2. *"I ask that my Higher Self work with my energetic fields and the guides to retrieve all responsibilities for connecting and loving my essence that I gave to others."*

3. *"I ask that all my reference points for connecting with my essence be brought back to my own divine line."*

4. *"I invite my Higher Self to work with my energetic fields and the guides to activate the vibration, sound, and light of my essence in my divine line at the level of my Higher Self."* Hold your awareness in your divine line. Imagine standing in a gentle and caressing waterfall of light.

5. Embrace your divine light. Acknowledge the beauty of your light.

6. As you appreciate the beauty, give yourself permission to love the light of your essence.

7. *"I invite my Higher Self to update all my reference points and all ways of perceiving my true self and all ways in which I am perceived by others."*

As you move through the day, hold awareness of the light that flows within you. Acknowledge that this is the true and perfect aspect of you. The more you hold your awareness in this place, the more you will act, speak, and move from a connected, beautiful, and powerful place.

FINDING PERFECTION BY CONNECTING WITHIN

Before my enlightenment experience, I was a type A perfectionist seeking external validation. I was never good enough. My solution was to push myself harder in every area of my life. Somehow, I believed that this would create a sense of perfection and fulfillment and the feeling that I was enough.

After my profound experience, I slowly learned that the only place I could feel fulfilled was in my divine line. Eventually I got the hang of it, and my new mantra became "Go inside for validation, perfection, and connection."

The road was bumpy during the first year. Insecurity was my unwelcome best friend. Fears that I was not good enough, smart enough, rich enough, powerful enough, skinny enough, pretty enough, or accomplished enough continually coursed through my heart and mind, like a gerbil on a wheel. After a year of watching and feeling these waves of insecurity, I finally decided to do something about it.

One late Friday afternoon after work, I felt the desire to take a romantic weekend with my beloved partner. He had not yet appeared in my physical life, but I had been dreaming about him and could energetically feel him in another realm.

It was early winter. The roads were clear, and the skies were blue. I packed an overnight bag, jumped in my car, cleared off the front seat for my higher-dimensional sweetheart, and headed for Taos, a six-hour drive from Telluride.

As I drove through the high desert in silence, I let my thoughts wander, watching them the way you would watch a dog chase its tail. My thoughts began the "I am not enough" cycle. "What if I meet him and he thinks I am annoying or too intense? I need to lose twenty pounds before I meet him. What if he doesn't think I am interesting? I should start educating myself on world events." As my all-too-familiar insecurities flew around me at lightning speed, I felt my angelic entourage appear in the backseat.

"Aleya, do you want to sit in your gerbil wheel of insecurity or flip it?" they asked.

"Can you show me how to flip it?" I responded.

The car started to fill with a white haze, and the energy began to spin within and around me. I slowed the car down and pulled over into a turnoff with a beautiful vista.

"Take a deep breath, and pull yourself into your divine line." As soon as my awareness was in my divine line, they continued.

"Can you see or feel the light flowing in your divine line?" they asked.

"A little bit," I said.

The guides continued: "Ask your Higher Self to work with your energetic fields to activate and amplify the light, sound, and vibration of your essence in your divine line at the level of your Higher Self."

I silently made the request to my Higher Self. From a distance, I watched my Higher Self do the work. I saw my guides encircling me and activating the vibration of their essence inside themselves. In a few moments, I found myself filled with a feeling of connection and perfection. My divine line expanded and got brighter.

"This light is your essence, Aleya. Explore it. Go deeper into the current," my guides gently urged me.

With each breath, I pulled my awareness into this inner river. It was beautiful and pure. I felt a deep peace and strength in this place.

"Can you embrace and love this light that is you?" my guides asked.

I thought to myself, "How do I love a river of light?"

Hearing my thoughts, my guides responded, "Recognize and appreciate the beauty within this light. Feel into all the amazing qualities that are held in this light."

As I recognized the beauty of my light more deeply, I felt a greater sense of appreciation and self-love. It felt peaceful, soothing, empowering, clear, and pure. The more I did this, the brighter and stronger the light glowed. I was in a state of awe at being in the presence of my own divine energy. Tears began to roll down my cheeks as a profound current of self-love rushed through me. I had never really taken the time to receive my own light for myself. I had been too wrapped up in the need for everyone else to receive and love me.

"Can you feel where you are enough and perfect in this place, Aleya?"

"Yes," I responded. As I held this inner awareness, my insecurity and fear of not being loved faded off into deep space.

"Bring all your reference points for your self-worth off of everything you do and off of all your outer accomplishments. Hold those reference points in direct connection to your light."

As my Higher Self pulled hundreds of reference points off others and outer accomplishments, I could feel a deep inner confidence and power building.

My guides continued, "Retrieve all responsibilities for seeing, embracing, and loving your essence. That is your job, and no one else's."

"I invite my Higher Self to work with my energetic fields to retrieve all responsibilities I have ever given to another for seeing and loving my essence," I silently requested.

Another wave of energy hit me as I felt this empowering responsibility return. I took a deep breath and opened my eyes. The world seemed brighter and lighter.

My guides spoke again, "Every time you feel insecure, fear rejection, or have thoughts that you are not enough, take a deep breath and feel the perfection and beauty of the light that is your essence and is always within you."

The mist in the car evaporated, and my backseat companions disappeared as they spoke their final words of wisdom.

When you tap into the beauty of your own inner light, you will experience a newfound power, connection, and confidence. Any time you have a moment of insecurity, use it as an opportunity to activate the vibration of self-love and self-worth in direct connection with your divine light. This is a healthy way of dealing with your insecurities; it will not be long before they are gone.

RELEASING INSECURITY

The specific protocol to help release any issues of insecurity and self-worth is the following: *"I invite the Higher Selves of me, my body deva, and my Team to work with the energetic fields and the guides to lift all reference points for our self-worth off of everyone and everything and bring them back to our individual divine lines. We ask that all responsibilities for validating our self-worth be retrieved. We ask for the activation of the vibration of self-love and self-worth in the divine lines of me, my body deva, and my Team."*

Take a deep breath in, and relax. Imagine the energetic aspects of you, your body deva, and your Team doing the work in the higher realms, and allow for this work to reflect into your life.

You may feel a shift in your body or a wave of relief. Emotions may rise up as the energy of insecurity or issues of self-worth lift up and out of your energy fields.

When you sense that the work has completed in the higher realms, finish the protocol with the following request: *"I ask that all our reference points and ways of perceiving be updated in all dimensions for me, my body deva, and my Team."*

When you directly align your self-worth with your divine light, issues of self-worth and insecurity will soon be far behind you.

HEALING LONELINESS WITH THE SEVENTH CUP

At different occasions in our lives — the holidays, divorce, infidelity, the death of a loved one or pet, the yearning for a beloved partner, or a relationship falling apart — loneliness can be an unwelcome guest. Despair, sadness, grief, depression, anger, abandonment, and a deep inner emptiness may consume you. When you seek connection externally, loneliness is bound to be right around the corner.

The Fourth Cup speaks to finding the solutions to challenges. In chapter 4 we learned that if loneliness is present, then connection is the solution. When you use the Fourth Cup — coupled with the Seventh — loneliness will fade.

Two years after I moved to Santa Barbara, my client Rebecca asked if I would treat her father. Six months earlier, her father had lost his wife in a tragic car accident. They had been married for twenty-eight years, and he was devastated by the loss. Since the death of his wife, Rebecca's father rarely left his home. He slept sixteen hours a day and was medicating himself with Scotch on the rocks, starting at 1:00 PM. Rebecca was understandably concerned.

I hesitated and then agreed. I remembered how I felt before I met my husband. On several occasions, I had been paralyzed by the loneliness and grief of not being able to find him.

On a foggy, cold Tuesday morning a week later, James walked into my office. I invited him to take a seat and explained how I work in my sessions.

James assured me that he and his wife had been into meditation and yoga for years and that my modality did not seem too "out there" for him.

When I asked him to share his intentions for the session, he didn't say much, other than that his grief was sometimes more than he could bear. He was not someone who wore his emotions on his sleeve. After a few minutes of conversation, I invited him to lie down on my water-filled sound table.

"Wow! I always wanted a waterbed, but I never got one. Maybe I should now," he added.

I placed my hands on his feet. A few moments later, I could feel the expansiveness of the higher realms. I focused on James's Higher Self and took several minutes to observe his energy. He looked as if he was frantically searching for someone.

I silently asked his Higher Self, "Who are you looking for?"

His Higher Self responded, "My wife, Susie."

Out loud, I said, "James, I was just checking in with your Higher Self. Up there, it seems as if you are looking for your wife. Does that resonate for you?"

Tears began to trickle down his cheeks. I handed him a tissue and said, "When people leave this physical world, they go into a different dimension. The energetic aspect of you has the ability to connect with her in this other realm. How would you feel about being able to energetically locate your wife where she exists now?"

He nodded his head and quietly said, "I don't know how to do that, but that would be really lovely, if it's even possible."

"Well, let's see. Shall we?"

I dropped back in, and up, to the higher planes of reality. "I am going to speak to your Higher Self. Would you like me to speak the protocol out loud?" I asked.

James told me he wanted to know what his energy self needed to do.

I held my awareness at the level of his Higher Self and made the following requests: "I invite your Higher Self, James, to work with your energetic fields and the guides to lift all your reference points off of your wife Susie's body deva, and to place your reference points for her on her light body energy self, which exists in a higher dimension."

I watched his Higher Self lift all his energetic locators out of the physical dimension and bring them up to a higher realm. I silently asked the guides to help his Higher Self locate Susie's light body in the higher realms.

As James's Higher Self located Susie's Higher Self, I continued, "I invite your Higher Self to connect with Susie at the level of her Higher Self in a way that is clean, clear, and supportive for both of you."

I watched James and Susie's Higher Selves connect with lines of light.

James sighed. Under his breath he said, "I can feel her."

I saw Susie's Higher Self in the higher realms, with her angelic advisers surrounding her. She was in her debrief. (A debrief is a life review that happens in the higher realms at the end of each life.) I took a moment to connect with Susie and her advisers. I let them know that James needed to update his reference points for Susie's energetic location. I asked Susie and her advisers if she was still holding any responsibilities that belonged to James.

I heard a yes and was guided to speak the following protocol: "Susie, at the level of your Higher Self, I invite you to return all responsibilities, Soul fragments belonging to James, and all relevant and appropriate information." I saw Susie send little energetic bundles to James's Higher Self.

I said, "James, at the level of your Higher Self, I invite you to return all responsibilities and any Soul fragments that belong to Susie, along with all relevant and appropriate information."

I watched this exchange of responsibilities for being loved, comforted, soothed, protected, supported, validated, and respected.

"I invite you, James, at the level of your Higher Self, to work with your energetic fields and the guides to lift all your gifts, wisdom, and mastery off of Susie and to place them back on yourself. I invite you to use your Soul's gifts to meet all your needs in your own divine line, instead of energetically looking to Susie to meet those needs. That is actually your job, regardless of the dimension Susie is in," I said gently.

As his Higher Self moved into action, I asked James how he was doing.

"More than anything, I feel lighter. Also, I did not realize I have been in a panicked state ever since Susie passed. This is the first time in six months that I have actually felt calm. I am not sure what is happening, but something's working," he reflected.

"This work is not for the mind. Nor does the mind do the work. Your Higher Self has the ability to shift your energy up high and reflect it into your consciousness and energetic fields. This shifts the way you feel."

James invited me to keep going.

I brought my awareness back up to the higher realms and scanned his Higher Self. He was calmer, and I was able to feel a greater flow of energy in his body, though I could still feel a pretty thick layer of grief and loneliness. I began looking for the root of his loneliness and flashed on an energy and image of James's mother. As I watched the scene unfold, I saw James around the age of six, clinging to his mom's leg. James's dad was screaming, and then he stormed out the front door and drove off in a fit of rage.

"James, what happened between your mother and father when you were around the age of six?" I asked.

"My father had an affair. My mother found out and confronted him. He packed his bags and left, never to return. She raised my brother and me on her own. She never remarried. I think it broke her heart."

"May I invite your Higher Self to release an energy that might not be yours regarding this situation and see if you feel any different? We might be able to release a level of grief and loneliness."

When James agreed, I said, "On a scale of one to ten, where are you in regards to your grief and loneliness?" I asked.

He closed his eyes and took a deep breath in. "I think I am at an eight."

"Okay. I am going to do the protocol. Then you can let me know how you feel," I instructed.

James nodded his head and closed his eyes. I closed my eyes too and brought my awareness back to my Higher Self and his. "I invite your Higher Self, your body deva, and your Team members to work with the energetic fields and the guides to energetically locate any grief or loneliness that belongs to your mother." I saw and felt his Higher Self collecting little dark balls of energy.

"I invite your Higher Self to return all emotions, issues, and karma that belong to your mother. Send those issues, lessons, and information to her at the level of her Higher Self, where she has the capacity to receive it in a way that empowers and serves her. Retrieve and use all your energetic tools, gifts, and wisdom on yourself and model that to her."

As I held James's feet and watched the work happen in the higher realms, a subtle vibration of joy began to emanate from him.

"I ask that all your reference points be updated. James, take a deep breath and think about that loneliness and grief. Where are you now on the scale?" I asked him.

He furrowed his brow and closed his eyes. I could feel him hunting around for those emotions. After a while he opened his eyes and gave me a confused smile.

"This is so weird. I can't believe it, but I am at a three. I can still feel a layer of grief for Susie, but I do not feel so abandoned and alone."

He closed his eyes as tears of relief ran down his cheeks. I handed him another tissue.

One session did not pull him out of his hole. It took James twelve sessions over a year, and a lot of hard inner work, to find a deep inner happiness and passion for life again. Within four years he was dating an amazing woman and had found a new community that was supportive and inspiring.

Everyone yearns for connection. If you look for connection internally in your divine line, you will create a more connected life. The more connected you are to the light that flows within you, the less loneliness you will experience.

If you use the Second Cup — "You Are Never Alone"— as well as the Seventh Cup, and activate the vibration of connection in your divine line, you may never feel loneliness again. If you use the Fourth Cup and use your loneliness challenge as an opportunity for growth, you will access a higher, more connected consciousness.

The other layer woven into James's story is holding the awareness that you can only shift your own issues, not someone else's. You do have useful information. Send the information, and return the issue. Let's talk more about how to do that.

LETTING GO OF ISSUES
THAT DON'T BELONG TO YOU

The greatest challenge of the Seventh Cup is the process of clearing away all the issues, lessons, and energy you are holding that do not belong to you. You can only shift your own issues. If you are holding the issues of another, they will not change, no matter how hard you try. James was holding an issue of his mother's.

That, coupled with the death of his wife, almost sank him into a bottomless pit. When you let go of the issues that do not belong to you, you will have enough energy and resources to work on your own.

Are there any struggles that you have been diligently trying to clear, to no avail? If so, they may not belong to you. You might be holding an ancestral issue or a former partner's issue. Regardless of who this issue might belong to, you can return it. Send any information you might have that can help whomever you are sending it to, and invite the energetic aspects of you, your body deva, and your Team to model the solution to the person(s) you may have been feeling.

I learned about this process while sitting in the backseat of my grandmother's car. My husband was driving us home from dinner. My grandmother was sitting in the front seat, making idle conversation with him. I was minding my own business, gazing up at the palm trees dancing in the light of the moon and smelling the warm ocean breeze.

Out of nowhere I was hit with a huge wave of grief. Within seconds I was a silent, sobbing mess. I took a deep breath in and flew up to my Higher Self to get a different angle. From that higher perspective, I looked down and saw a dark cloud coming from my grandmother. This cloud was filled with all the lessons and issues she had not yet completed. For some reason she thought that she could hand them off to me.

I immediately connected with her Higher Self and informed her that those were her lessons, not mine.

Her Higher Self responded, "Yes, well, I am about to die, and I just thought you could work on them for me."

I continued the silent higher-dimensional conversation. "I am happy to send you any information I have regarding your lessons, but you are the only one who has the capacity to shift this energy. I know you have a deep wisdom and capacity to continue your evolution, even on the other side."

She begrudgingly nodded, and I made a silent request. "I invite my Higher Self to work with my energetic fields and the guides to send you all the information I have that can help you in your growth, evolution, and transition."

I held my awareness at the level of our Higher Selves for a few minutes as I sent the energetic information.

When I saw her Higher Self receive it, I continued, "I invite my Higher Self to return all fragments, issues, responsibilities, karma, and lessons that belong to you, my grandmother."

I saw the dark balls of energy lift off of me and return to her at the place where she was able to work on them in her own unique way. As soon as I returned the responsibility for shifting her issues, my grief lifted. I wiped my tears away with the back of my hand, took a deep breath in, and swallowed a large cup of humility, which slowly became a brew of wisdom.

Seven weeks later, my grandmother died. I was able to feel her new location as she held her consciousness in her light body. Instead of feeling grief and loss, I felt excitement for the next phase of her journey and celebrated her graduation into a higher plane. I could have been consumed with grief and frustration, had I kept my grandmother's bundle of issues.

Connecting with your essence becomes effortless once you release the issues and trauma picked up in the womb and during your childhood, and that may have been unconsciously handed to you by your ancestors or other people in your life.

When you hold the issues of others, you may feel less than perfect. Over time, you may forget what your own essence feels like. This challenge usually sets in between the ages of seven and fourteen, sometimes earlier, depending on your exposure to traumatic events. When you let go of energies that are not yours, you will be able to feel your essence again.

RELEASING ISSUES THAT ARE NOT YOURS

Here is the protocol to help you release the issues that you are holding that are not yours: *"I invite the Higher Selves of me, my body deva, and my Team to work with our energetic fields and the guides to locate all issues, lessons, challenges, karma, power, and energy that do not belong to us and to return it back to its right and perfect place, along with all relevant energetic information."*

Complete the protocol with this request: *"We ask that all our reference points and ways of perceiving be updated."*

As you let go of issues that are not yours, you will be able to use your energy far more efficiently. You may need to use this specific protocol many times before you feel a complete clearing. You might want to break it up into three parts. Hold space and focus on your Higher Self releasing the issues that do not belong to you. Then hold space and walk your body deva through the steps. Do the same thing for your Team members. The more slowly you go through a protocol, the deeper it penetrates.

INSIGHTS AND THINGS TO REMEMBER

- You are a beautiful and perfect beam of light having an experience in the physical human form.
- The light of your essence is flawless, perfect, and unique and can never be tainted or destroyed.
- Your primary responsibility is to love the light of your essence, which flows in your divine line.
- You are the only one who can deeply connect with your essence.
- You are the only one who is in your divine line.
- All your energetic needs flow in your divine line.

- The only place where you will find and feel a true and deep connection is inside your divine line.
- A Soul who embraces its own divine light will have different belief systems than a Soul who is immersed in a perception of disconnection. Hold your awareness in your divine line.
- You can only shift your own issues, not another's.
- The more you hold your awareness in your divine line, the more your consciousness evolves.

The How

Let's dive into the spiritual lab and practice the quick steps for connecting to your essence. Then we'll practice the full protocol for releasing issues that are not yours.

The Quick Protocol

Take a deep breath in. Use your inhale, intent, Higher Self, and energetic fields to pull all your awareness and energy into your divine line. Hold your awareness in your inner river of light, and snuggle up on the front of your spine. Ask your Higher Self to activate the vibration of your essence in your divine line. Recognize, embrace, and appreciate this amazing and beautiful light. Invite your body deva and your Team to do the same. Update your reference points.

The Full Protocol

1. Find a comfortable place to sit or lie down.
2. Take a few deep breaths into your belly. Use your inhale

to pull all your energy out of the future and back into the present breath. Use your exhale to pull all your energy out of the past and back into the breath of now.

3. Once you are in the present moment *(you can only shift your consciousness when you are in the present moment)*, use your inhale to pull yourself into your divine line. Out loud or silently repeat the following: *"I invite my Higher Self to work with my energetic fields and the guides to pull all my energy, anchors, reference points, and awareness off of everyone and everything and back to my divine line."* Take a moment to feel the shift, and let your Higher Self do the work.

4. *"I invite my Higher Self to work with my energetic fields and the guides to firmly attach my divine line to the front of my spine."* Before you travel into another dimension, put your anchor down by firmly attaching to the front of your spine. You will be much safer that way. Your body deva will appreciate this as well.

5. Holding your awareness in your divine line, either stay in your divine line on the front of your spine, or travel up your column of light (crystal elevator shaft) to your Higher Self. Say the following: *"I ask my Higher Self to work with my energetic fields and the guides to locate all issues, karma, and lessons that I am holding for my ancestors, descendants, lovers, friends, colleagues, teachers, healers, or humanity. I ask that all these issues and energies be returned to their right and perfect place. I ask that all relevant and appropriate information be relayed to them at the level of their Higher Selves, where they have the capacity to receive the energy and the information."* Take a few minutes, and hold awareness that your Higher Self is working up high and unloading the issues that are not yours,

as well as sending the information to all the people you were trying to help. When you carry an issue that is not yours, you end up disempowering others. Instead, practice seeing others' courage and wisdom to shift their own issues in their unique ways. What they really need from you is information and for you to hold the solution and model it to them. Your mind will not know the specific energetic information. Just ask your Higher Self to send it, whatever that information may be.

6. Lift your gifts, wisdom, and mastery back to you (Sixth Cup). Say the following: *"I invite my Higher Self to work with my energetic fields and the guides to retrieve all my gifts, wisdom, mastery, and energetic tools off of everyone and everything. I invite my Higher Self to clean, clear, and realign my gifts and to use them on me."* Doing this will help you model the solution to others. Take a moment, and let the work happen at the level of your Higher Self.

7. *"I invite my Higher Self to work with my energetic fields and the guides to release all empathic sensitivity, thought forms, emotions, behaviors, and karma that are not mine."*

8. Invite your body deva and your Team to do the same: *"I invite my body deva and my Team at the level of their Higher Selves to work with their energetic fields and the guides to locate all issues, karma, and lessons that they are holding for any ancestors, decedents, lovers, friends, colleagues, teachers, healers, or humanity from all incarnations, and to return all these issues and energy back to their right and perfect places, along with all relevant and appropriate information to everyone at the level of their Higher Selves, where they have the capacity to receive the information. I invite my body deva and my Team to retrieve all their gifts, wisdom, mastery, and energetic tools off of*

everyone and everything. I ask that these gifts be cleaned, cleared, and realigned for my body deva and my Team, so they can hold and use these resources for themselves and model that energy to others." Hold awareness as the Higher Selves of your body deva and your Team do the work in the higher realms.

9. *"I invite the Higher Selves of me, my body deva, and my Team to activate the vibration of our unique essence in our individual divine lines."* Breathe, wait, and allow. Imagine opening vertically and internally to receive the light and sound of your essence. Be the flower to the sun. Imagine a stream of light flowing vertically inside you, up and down. Imagine standing under a gentle, pure waterfall of light. Invite the light to flow down through the top of your head and down the front of your spine. Invite your body deva to be open to receiving its pure essence light in its own divine line.

10. You can imagine the light flowing up and/or down your divine line. It flows both ways. At first, just imagine your light flowing down from your divine spark, which resides in the divine Source energy. As you get more comfortable, play with the flow in your divine line. Feel it gently moving in both directions, up and down. The energy may flow more easily down than up, and you may also be able to empathically feel the energy going up or down the divine line of your body deva.

Do what feels right for you. Go slowly. Always ask your Higher Self to do the work, not your mind. If you force things with your mind, the flow of energy may become uncomfortable, or maybe nothing will happen at all.

Also, make sure to always flow your light vertically, up and down, not horizontally. If you do direct your light horizontally, you will quickly overwhelm and blow out others. People will be less inclined to hang out with you. (I learned that the hard way.) Think of your divine line like a fire hose. It is powerful.

11. When you release issues that are not yours, you will begin to hold a higher vibration. You can use the following protocol to help you and your body deva adjust to a higher frequency: *"I invite my body deva to work with its energetic fields and the guides to balance the electrical and magnetic energy within and around the spinal fluid and within the microbes. I invite the Higher Selves of me, my body deva, and my Team to release all negative karma at this higher level, to scan this higher energetic terrain, and to orient to this higher energetic way of being from a place of balance, safety, clarity, empowerment, support, gratitude, and humility."*

12. You just moved to a new level. Take a few moments to let that energetic aspect of you adjust and get used to this new terrain. The protocol above can also help alleviate "ascension headaches."

Update your reference points and all ways in which you perceive. Reset your energetic compass: "I invite all the reference points for me, my body deva, and my Team to be updated, as well as all the ways in which I perceive and am perceived in all realms."

Take a few deep breaths, and check in with yourself. Do you feel the same? Do you feel lighter? Calmer? Freer? Happier? Clearer? More grounded? More relaxed? If you feel heavier, you might actually be feeling grounded. If you feel tired, you might be feeling relaxed. Sometimes when we're not used to these feelings, we don't recognize them.

When you let go of energy that does not belong to you, you may feel a combination of relief, lightness, and fatigue. Imagine hiking for eight hours and then taking your seventy-pound pack off your back. You will feel light as a feather and beyond exhausted. Allow for the process of integration and rest.

SEVENTH CUP AUDIO MEDITATIONS

To listen to the audio meditations for the Seventh Cup, go to www.cupsofconsciousness.com/meditations.

Connecting with and Loving the Light of Your Essence and Releasing Issues That Are Not Yours

This meditation will help you hold all your reference points in your divine line and connect with the aspect of you that is perfect. Energetically locate all issues that do not belong to you, your body deva, or your Team, and send them back to their right and perfect place.

> *Deep within you runs a beautiful river of light.*
> *This light carries the vibration of your essence,*
> *which is perfect, connected, and whole.*

Empathic Sensitivity

*C*ongratulations! You have sipped from all seven cups, but there is still one more vital area to cover: empathic sensitivity. This is not a cup but rather a concept that flows through all the cups.

Empathic sensitivity means feeling the emotions, hearing the thoughts, or having an energetic, emotional, or physical experience of another. It can be a blessing or a curse.

It is a curse when you are reactive to feelings that are not yours and when you are not even aware that they aren't yours. It is a blessing if you are conscious of your empathic sensitivity and have the tools for clearing the sensations and modeling the solutions to others.

Conscious empathic sensitivity helps you know what another person is experiencing. You energetically walk a mile in their shoes, so to speak. Knowing others' challenges will help you model the solution to them, and feeling the pain of another is the fastest way to cultivate compassion. The trick is not to take responsibility for fixing the pain and instead to have compassion for the person who is suffering and to model the solution.

The more evolved you become, the more sensitive you will be and the more compassion you will want to cultivate. Highly evolved beings are extremely compassionate. They do not take responsibility for the pain of others. They are not attached to being the fixer. They hold the safest space and model the solution in their own energy fields. The moment the one who is suffering feels safe, she or he will connect to her or his own healing source and start to energetically shift and heal. This happens automatically when someone energetically and emotionally feels safe.

You are only responsible for your own inner energy. If you are a caregiver of any kind, do make dinner and offer support, but make sure you are not taking responsibility for your charge's energetic reality. This stance is healthier and more empowering for everyone involved.

ENERGETIC SENSITIVITY

Thousands of years ago, human beings developed empathic sensitivity as a survival mechanism. The ability to know what someone else was feeling or experiencing created the capacity for cooperation when we were hunters and gatherers. Physiologically the human body developed mirror neurons in the brain that allowed us to experience the emotions of another. Reading the emotions of another person is both energetic and physiological. Energetically, your empathic capacity continues to evolve as your consciousness expands.

Think about the energetic sixth sense that you've been developing. Do you energetically hear, see, feel, smell, or taste? Whatever your strongest sense is will be the aspect of you that is most empathic.

After my enlightenment experience, my awareness amplified

a thousandfold. For the first three years I was assaulted by the outside world. I was able to hear other people's thoughts, feel their feelings, and experience what was going on in their bodies. For days, sometimes weeks, I would feel another person's emotional or physical pain. It was brutal.

It took everything in me not to be reactive or medicate with antianxiety drugs or pain pills. As I thrashed about, knowing that what I was feeling was not my own, I forced myself to examine every layer. I was determined to maintain my sanity and inner peace and to stay drug free. So I developed energetic tools and concepts that helped me navigate all those empathic feelings.

After a decade of unpacking the empathic experience, I have created specific steps that will help you use your empathic sensitivity to develop greater compassion, less reactivity, greater discernment, and the ability to move into healthier relationships with others.

The solution for dealing with empathic sensitivity is using a combination of the Third, Fourth, Sixth, and Seventh Cups. There are six factors to keep in mind as you gather the tools to help you gracefully navigate empathic sensitivity.

The first aspect is discernment. The second is sending energetic information to whomever you are feeling. The third aspect is holding appropriate attachment. The fourth is personal responsibility. The fifth is modeling right energy/the solution. And the six and final aspect is holding compassion and a safe space for the person you are empathically feeling.

Developing Discernment

A lack of discernment is one of the greatest challenges of having empathic sensitivity. For when you lack discernment, you will perceive emotions and sensations and think they are yours. If you are merrily skipping through the grocery store and suddenly get hit with a wave of anger or a headache that literally comes out of nowhere, you have just landed in the realm of empathic sensitivity.

If you are getting ready to go see a friend and you feel a huge wave of grief that comes "out of nowhere," you may very likely be feeling the emotions of the friend you are about to visit.

Empathic sensitivity usually comes up suddenly, but not always. The trick is to be aware and have a reference point for your true state. The more familiar you become with the energy that flows in your divine line, the more discernment you will gain regarding empathic sensitivity. Spend time in your divine line and feel the quality of the energy flowing there. You can also use the connecting with your essence meditation in chapter 7.

Sending Energetic Information

The second factor when dealing with empathic sensations is realizing that the moment you feel an empathic sensation, that is an indicator that you have information for whomever you are feeling. Invite your Higher Self, your body deva's Higher Self, and your Team's Higher Selves to send appropriate energetic information to the person's Higher Self. Ask that the information be sent to them where they have the capacity to receive it in an empowering and supportive way.

You do not need to mentally know the specifics of the energetic information. Let the Higher Selves of you, your body deva, and your Team make that determination.

Often I ask the Higher Selves of me, my body deva, and my Team to send the information to the person I am feeling, and the empathic sensation instantly clears. If it does not clear, I address the aspects of attachment and responsibility.

Holding Appropriate Attachment

Appropriate attachment, and the next aspect, responsibility, go hand in hand. The moment you become attached to someone else's reality, in the next breath you will unconsciously and energetically take responsibility for his reality. This creates an energetically confused state that is often called "codependence."

The more attached you are to your own behavior and emotions, as opposed to those of other people, the less empathically reactive you will be. Hold space for people to be however they need to be, as you model a connected, loving energy.

If you feel attached to someone's emotional state or behavior, invite your Higher Self to get busy. Ask the Higher Selves of you, your body deva, and your Team to use the energetic fields to retrieve all the energetic attachment nuggets that you have placed on another. Ask that all your attachment be held in your own divine line, and the same goes for your body deva and your Team.

Above all else, be attached to the light that flows in your divine line. This energetic stance will also help you stay connected to your essence and to model a healthy stance to others.

Taking Responsibility

As you, your body deva, and your Team hold your attachment on yourselves, you are ready to address the next layer, responsibility. Invite the Higher Selves of you, your body deva, and your Team to return all the energetic responsibilities you are holding for another. Let others be energetically responsible for their own emotions and behavior.

Imagine what it feels like when someone takes responsibility for a task that belongs to you. It can be very disempowering and in some instances insulting. When you return all energetic responsibility to someone, as well as sending any information that you have that could help her, she becomes empowered.

Modeling Right Energy

As you hold appropriate attachment and responsibility, you are ready for the next step: holding your tools, gifts, and wisdom on yourself. When you empathically feel someone else, you will unconsciously or consciously want to help. This desire triggers a pattern of energetically placing your gifts on the person you are feeling (Sixth Cup). You may try to use your energy to soothe, control, or change that person. This does not actually help him or her, and it can deplete you.

Instead, invite the Higher Selves of you, your body deva, and your Team to lift all your gifts, tools, wisdom, and mastery off of the person you are feeling. Hold these resources on yourself, and model a healthier way of being.

The people you are empathic with actually want to know how you do what you do at an energetic level. Teach them to fish instead of giving them a fish…

Holding a Compassionate and Safe Space

As you model right energy or the solution inside yourself, always hold a safe, compassionate stance. You were just feeling another person's reality — it probably was not a comfortable experience. The person you are feeling may not have the tools that you are learning about in these pages. So it is time for you to increase compassion and to hold a safe space. Let the other be however he or she needs to be. Be attached to and responsible for only your internal reality, not another's. Send information, and model the solution. Take a deep breath, and check to see if you are still feeling the empathic sensation. When you feel neutral, or the emotion is no longer present or triggered, you have successfully cleared the empathic sensation.

It took me years to figure out all the steps. It used to take me hours, sometimes days, to clear the empathic emotions and sometimes the physical pain that belonged to others. Now it takes me just a few minutes.

When you are clearing an empathic sensation, remember to focus on your Higher Self and to hold space for the Higher Selves of your body deva and your Team as well. It may be affecting one or all three.

If you are physically feeling an empathic sensation, such as hip pain or a headache, that is an indicator that your body deva has information for someone else's body deva. Invite the Higher Self of your body deva to recognize that what it is feeling does not belong to it. Ask that your body deva use its Higher Self and energetic fields to send appropriate information to whomever it is feeling. Ask your body deva to lift all attachment off the other body deva, return all responsibility, retrieve all gifts and energetic tools, and model the solution. Ask your body deva to hold a safe and compassionate space for the other body deva in the higher realms.

Once your body deva's Higher Self has completed those steps, ask that all reference points be updated.

DETERMINING THE ORIGIN OF EMPATHIC SENSATIONS

I believe that about 80 percent of our thoughts and feelings may actually be coming from someone else. While it sounds extreme, grasping this concept can actually come as a relief.

The first step in discerning the origin of your sensations is to determine if what you are feeling is indeed yours or if it belongs to another. If you know without a doubt that the sensations are empathic and belong to another, you can dive deeper and find the specific origin, or you can simply skip ahead and use the protocol to clear empathic sensations.

To determine if your sensations belong to you or to someone else, you can use the following techniques.

Whose Feelings Are These?

Ask your Higher Self to check if what you are feeling is yours or someone else's: *"I ask my Higher Self to determine if what I am feeling is mine."* Hold space for your Higher Self to discern the origin and send the answer to you. If you do not get clarity using this technique, you can muscle test or use a pendulum, or you can get two blank note cards and write "mine" on one and "someone else's" on the other. (Muscle testing uses the strength of your muscles to determine a yes or no response. A pendulum is an object that dangles from a cord and will spin in a clockwise or counterclockwise direction when a question is asked. A pendulum and muscle testing will only give you a yes or no response. You can check out YouTube to learn how to muscle test and use a pendulum.)

The feeling you are experiencing might actually be yours, which means it is not empathic. To heal your own issues, you will need to go back to the Fourth Cup, identifying the challenge and determining the solution. You can refer to the Flip-It section online and to chapter 4 for help in shifting your issues.

Once you have determined that the sensation is not yours, you can hone in on it and find its specific origin. There are three possible sources; it may be coming from a Team member, from your body deva, or from another source.

If it is another source and you want to know the specific origin of an empathic sensation, I recommend creating note cards or using my empathic deck. Online I provide a complete list of nineteen other possible origins (www.cupsofconsciousness/meditations).

You do not have to mentally know the specific origin of an empathic sensation. You can simply invite the Higher Selves of you, your body deva, and your Team to locate the origin in the higher realms.

You can use the following steps to help you find the origin of the empathic sensation or determine if it belongs to you.

1. Find a quiet space.
2. Take a few deep breaths, close your eyes, and bring your awareness into your divine line.
3. Drop into your heart, and increase your willingness and courage to see the deepest root of whatever emotion, sensation, or issue you may be feeling at the time.
4. Ask your Higher Self to locate the origin of this empathic sensation.
5. If you have an empathic deck, flip through the cards and ask for the deepest root of the possible empathic energy to be revealed. (I have an empathic deck that you can get on my website, http://bit.ly/1Gh9HQ6.)
6. Ask your Higher Self to reveal the origin, or simply read the card you pulled.

Once you have determined the source of the empathic sensation, assuming it is not yours, you are ready to practice the full protocol at the end of this chapter. Before we dive into the how, let's take a moment to review.

Insights and Things to Remember

- Empathic sensitivity is the ability to feel, hear, or know the experiences, feelings, or thoughts of another.
- Learn to discern when you are feeling another person's reality.
- You can only shift your own emotions, sensations, and issues. If something does not shift, it most likely belongs to another person.
- People begin to heal and evolve when they feel they are in a safe and loving space.

- As you clear your empathic sensations, remember that your Higher Self and your energy fields are doing the work, not your mind. Use your mind to make the request, and then sit like a bump on a log and wait for the work to happen in the higher realms.
- When the work is complete in the higher realms, you will feel an inner shift. It may be a twitch, a sigh, or a body wiggle, and then you will feel the release of the empathic emotion.
- When issues clear or empathic sensations release, you may literally feel them lifting up and out of your energy fields. Let the energy release and lift out. Think of it like sweating, exhaling, or doing your business. Let it go. Do not resist the release. That will cause discomfort.
- If it does not shift, sit in stillness for a moment. Sometimes it takes twenty seconds to feel the clearing; sometimes several hours.
- At first this work is subtle, but the more you do it, the more obvious the shifts become.

The How

Let's dive into the spiritual lab, where you can use the quick steps or the full protocol for clearing empathic sensitivity.

The Quick Steps

Hold awareness of the sensation you are feeling. Discern whether it is yours. If it comes out of nowhere, it most likely is not. Hold your attachment and desire on yourself. Release the energetic responsibility you are holding for another. Send the appropriate energetic information to the place where it has the capacity to be received. Bring your gifts back on yourself and off of others. Model the solution. Hold compassion and a safe space for the person you were feeling. Use the quick protocol below to clear empathic sensations.

THE QUICK SPECIFIC EMPATHIC SENSITIVITY PROTOCOL

"I invite the Higher Selves of me, my body deva, and my Team to work with our energetic fields and the guides to send all information and responsibility that we may be holding to whomever we are feeling, to the place where they have the capacity to receive it. We ask that all our attachment and gifts be lifted off of them and brought back to us, where we have the capacity to hold them and to model the solution in our fields. At the level of our Higher Selves we ask to hold a container of safety and compassion for the person we were feeling. We ask that all our reference points and all ways of perceiving be updated."

Take a breath, and imagine those energetic aspects of you, your body deva, and your Team doing this work. Be attached to and responsible for your own energy in your own divine line, model the solution, and hold compassion.

The more you practice this protocol, the more quickly your empathic sensations will clear. Really focus on the component of compassion, which is vital in clearing empathic sensitivity. Holding a compassionate space for someone is the most healing thing you can do.

The Full Protocol

1. Increase your awareness of the feelings or sensations you are experiencing.
2. Practice discernment. Hold the awareness that this may not be your energy but an empathic experience.
3. Bring your awareness into your divine line, and make the following requests.
4. *"I invite the Higher Selves of me, my body deva, and my Team to lift all our desires, wants, and attachment off of the person we are empathically feeling."*
5. Hold all your desires, wants, and attachment on yourself, not on another. Only want for your own self. (Example: I desire only for my own happiness, not another person's happiness.) This is heresy in our codependent culture. But if you want to hold a really strong energy field, you have to start by being attached to your own energy, not that of others. Then you can model that energy of inner happiness to others.
6. *"I invite the Higher Selves of me, my body deva, and my Team to return all energetic responsibility for changing another person's reality back to him or her at the level of his or her Higher Self, where he or she has the capacity to hold it."*
7. *"I ask that we retrieve all our Soul's gifts and resources off of the other and bring them back to ourselves."* Use your gifts on yourself; the same goes for your body deva and Team.
8. *"I ask the Higher Selves of me, my body deva, and my Team to send whatever energetic information we have for the other person. Send it to him or her at the level of his or her Higher Self, body deva's Higher Self, and Team."*
9. Model the solution for what you think this person needs. Hold a safe, compassionate, nonfixing, nonjudging space.

Let this person be in the energy he or she is choosing consciously or unconsciously.

EMPATHIC CUP AUDIO MEDITATIONS

To listen to the audio meditations for clearing empathic sensations, go to www.cupsofconsciousness.com/meditations.

Clearing Empathic Sensitivity

This meditation will help the Higher Self of you, your body deva, and your Team locate the sensation you are experiencing. Lift all your attachment off of others, and bring it back to yourself. Return all responsibilities. Lift your gifts off others. Send appropriate information. Model the solution to the person you were empathically feeling. Hold compassion and a safe space for this person in the higher realms.

Helping Your Body Deva Clear Empathic Sensitivity

This meditation will help your body deva release all empathic sensations and model right energy to the other body deva it is feeling.

May you model right energy and hold
compassion as you move through your day
and as you sleep, dream, and play.

Conclusion:
Sipping from All the Cups

*W*hen you sip from the cups every day, your life becomes full. Your Team and guides help you in every breath. You shift your inner world by using your Higher Self. You use every challenge as a lesson to propel you into a conscious state of divine connection. Your body deva evolves and cultivates greater self-love, inner peace, self-control, and health. In every breath, you use the tools you have cultivated for yourself. You model a powerful field of coherence to others. And last but not least, you experience deep self-love and awe when you connect with your essence. As your life transforms, be grateful for your inner work as it reflects into the outer world.

The energetic aspects of you, your body, and your Team are vital resources. Your energy will become more robust the more you use these dimensional resources. Imagine using these concepts for a year. Your inner life will shift and will reflect the flow, abundance, and connection you have cultivated internally. Be patient. It may take a few weeks, months, or even years for the changes to appear in your outer world.

Using the Cups and Making Them Your Own

When you use all seven cups, you will experience a greater sense of support. Each cup helps you understand why your life is the way it is and provides the tools for changing it. You can use the tools embedded in each cup to help you clear your blocks. Your behavior will align with your intentions. Your inner struggles will release as you, your body deva, and your Team all head in the same direction. When you work with the cups, keep the following in mind.

Connecting with your essence may feel unfamiliar at first. Take the time to hold your awareness in your divine line. The more time you spend in your divine line, the more comfortable you will be with the divine aspect of you. You will also begin to feel a stronger sense of self-love, connection, inner sacredness, and safety in your core.

Ask your Team members to buffer and model right energy to you. They can be an incredible support system. The more you ask them to help you, the more help you will receive. Focus on cultivating a healthy, cocreative relationship with them. Ask your Team members to be responsible for their own energy. Ask them to meet their own needs internally by activating the desired vibrations in their divine lines.

Help your body deva awaken by recognizing its unique nature consciousness. Firmly attach your divine line to the front of your spine. You will be more grounded and supported. Love the light that flows in your divine line. Model that to your body deva. Invite your body deva to love the light of its essence. Ask your body deva to use all its resources for manifesting what it desires. Your body deva *loves* to create. Give it full responsibility for manifesting.

As you, your body deva, and your Team use your wisdom, your resources will bloom. As you appreciate your wisdom, you will be appreciated in the world.

Think of every challenge as the next rung on your spiritual ladder. You will become more conscious every time you flip your challenge into a lesson. Over time, your challenges will decrease, and you will be propelled into greater empowerment. You have the tools to change your inner life. As with all tools, you need to pick them up and use them.

If you feel pulled to explore one cup in particular, go for it. Leave all the other cups, and dive into the one that calls to you. As you spiritually evolve, your desire to sip from different cups will change. Your curiosity is your best guide and will lead you to the appropriate cup.

There are specific practices within each cup that can help you make the changes you intend. As you sip on the concepts, use the tools, and do the protocols, you will attain the particular internal and external realities you desire. For example, if you want to experience greater inner peace and connection, use the Seventh Cup.

- Each day take three conscious breaths, and pull yourself into your divine line.
- As you move through your day, imagine holding a little more of your awareness in your divine line.
- Ask your Higher Self to activate the vibration of peace and connection in your divine line. Imagine a little current of peace and connection flowing vertically in your divine line.
- Ask your body deva and your Team to do the same in their divine lines.

If you want greater support and abundance in your life, use the Sixth Cup.

- Invite the Higher Selves of you, your body deva, and your Team to retrieve and use all your wisdom, tools, and gifts.

- Ask your Higher Self to activate the vibration of support in your divine line. Invite your body deva and your Team to do the same. The more you find your support in your divine line, the more supported you will be in your life.

You can also use the Second Cup to increase the support in your life.

- Ask your Team members to encircle you and be your buffer.
- Ask them to increase their own boundaries.
- Ask them to increase their inner vibrations of support, empowerment, and safety and to model that to you.

If you want a healthier body, use the Fifth Cup.

- Every morning acknowledge your body deva. Say, "Good morning, body deva."
- Ask your body deva to hold responsibility for loving the light that flows in its divine line.
- Invite your body deva to control itself.
- Firmly attach your divine line to the front of your spine.
- Ask your Higher Self to activate the vibration of vitality and balance in your divine line, and model that to your body deva.

Here are some more suggestions to help you sip from the cups.

For the next six months:

- Every morning say, "Good morning, Team" (Second Cup).

- Pick one challenge, and for two weeks, ask the Higher Selves of you, your body deva, and your Team to resolve it in the higher realms (Third and Fourth Cups).
- Once a week, ask the Higher Selves of you, your body deva, and your Team to retrieve all responsibilities for meeting your own needs. Meet your needs in your divine line. Find your safety, love, and connection in your divine line (First and Second Cups).
- On the new moon, ask the Higher Selves of you, your body deva, and your Team to retrieve all energetic tools and gifts. Use your gifts on yourself (First, Second, and Sixth Cups).
- Take thirty seconds each day to hold your awareness in your divine line. Invite your body deva and your Team to do the same (Seventh Cup).

Using the Protocols

By now you have learned that most of the work is done through using the protocols in the higher realms. The Higher Selves of you, your body deva, and your Team do the steps within the protocols. Your Higher Self shifts and reflects those changes from the higher realms into this realm.

If you observe closely, you will discover that each step of each protocol pulls from a cup or a combination of cups.

When you formulate a protocol, keep in mind the following steps so that you can create your own.

1. Acknowledge that you are a multidimensional being. Use your resources in the other dimensions, and call on your guides and Team (First and Second Cups): "*I ask the Higher Selves of me, my body deva, and my Team to work with the energetic fields and the guides to...*"

2. Identify the energy you wish to shift. Shift your inner world to change your outer world (Third Cup): *"Locate the energy of (fear, lack, and so on)."*

3. Flip it. Use your challenge to grow and evolve (Fourth Cup): *"Activate the vibration of trust."*

4. Invite your body deva to hold the higher vibration for itself (Fifth Cup): *"I invite my body deva to do the same at the level of its Higher Self and in its divine line."*

5. Hold and use your gifts, wisdom, and mastery for yourself, and model that in the world (Sixth Cup): *"As you hold the vibration of trust in your divine lines, you can model that in the world."*

6. Update your reference points, and hold more of your awareness on the light that flows in your divine line (Seventh Cup): *"We ask that all our reference points be updated, as well as all the ways in which we perceive and are perceived."*

The protocols can be powerful, so go slowly. Remember, let your Higher Self absorb, reflect, and digest the cups. When you let your Higher Self extract what you need, your mind will receive and understand the wisdom.

USING THE AUDIO MEDITATIONS

You can use the audio meditations as a stand-alone practice or as a warm-up before your own meditation. The meditations work directly with your Higher Self and energy fields, not your mind. An ancient and wise eight-year-old once said to me, "Aleya, when I listen to your meditations, I do not listen. I just feel it. It works much better that way."

FINAL REMINDERS

- The three components of the sacred trinity — you, your body deva, and your Team — all need to hold a similar vibration so that your issues can clear and you can manifest your intentions.
- Get in your divine line before you make a request to your Higher Self.
- Make requests of the Higher Selves of you, your body deva, and your Team. Let the work happen in the higher realms.
- Your Higher Self shifts you. In this way you stay in your power instead of having someone else do the work "to" you.
- If the energy feels too intense, ask your Higher Self to slow down and be gentler. Ask your Higher Self to adjust the energetic volume down or up, depending on your comfort level.
- Use your Higher Self and your energy fields to change your consciousness and behaviors and to release your blocks.
- You can only shift your own issues, not the issues of others.
- Remind your body deva to shift its energy using the higher realms. As your Soul evolves, you will be able to assist your body in its own evolution as well. Invite your body deva to awaken and hold a higher consciousness.
- Use your empathic sensitivity to master compassion and to model the solution to the person you were feeling.
- Take responsibility for your own awakening. Use your Higher Self as your primary mechanism for growth and evolution, instead of the outer world.
- Update your reference points after every protocol.

You never go backward in your evolution. For ten years, I have been practicing and teaching these concepts. I have watched my own life shift dramatically and have personally seen hundreds of lives transform in beautiful ways.

As you access higher states of consciousness, I hope that the cups will support and inspire you. As you sip from them, your life will change. It is inevitable. Perhaps your life has already started to change as you have been reading this book. Get ready for even bigger changes as you hold greater connection, flow, support, safety, and love in your divine line.

As you awaken, no matter what changes come, hold the stance that every change is moving you toward greater happiness, service, connection, and love.

May your journey be filled with all that you desire,
as you hold that same energy in your own divine line.

Acknowledgments

I would like to thank New World Library for embracing the cups; my agent, Devra Jacobs, for reminding me that not everyone has an angelic Bluetooth headset; Rebecca Stinson, my PR guru, for laughing and crying while reading my rough draft; Sue Denniston, for the amazing online images of my terms; Krista Kieding, for being the best fairy on my editing assembly line and for moving me into the slingshot position; Freckles, my constant companion, who demanded many walks to help me keep my head clear during the endless hours of writing and rewriting; the good organic coffee that kept me grounded while I was going into altered states while writing; Doug Noll, my beloved husband, for his love and support and for editing this book with gentleness and love; Robinson Eikenberry, for teaching me about detail, focus, and patience; George Friedenthal for the incredible background music on the meditations and all the support; my sweet mom, who has always held a space of love and support in all that I do; and my spiritual family, Team, and guides on the other side who sing to me and whisper words of love and wisdom.

To all the students and clients who contributed their stories and helped me delve deeper into the concepts that made this book possible; to all the Cups of Consciousness subscribers who for years have asked me to share my story in written form; and to you, for inspiring me in the higher realms and for holding a space for me to reflect to you your own wisdom:

Thank you.

Audio Meditations

*T*o listen to the audio meditations in this book, go to www
.cupsofconsciousness/meditations.

1. First Cup: You Live in a Multidimensional Reality
   Connecting to Your Divine Line
   Connecting with Your Higher Self
   Activating Your Blueprints
   Taking Connected Conscious Breaths

2. Second Cup: You Are Never Alone
   Connecting with Your Team

3. Third Cup: You Can Change Your Inner World
   Activating Your Desired Vibrations in Your Divine Line

4. Fourth Cup: Your Challenges Can Help You Grow
   Using Your Challenges to Grow

Online Resources

Yoou can find more about me and the resources I offer at www.aleyadao.com.

For a free week of daily Cups of Consciousness and a free sample of a Tall Cups session, go to www.cupsofconsciousness.com.

If you want to start slowly by taking little sips of the cups, you can receive the daily Cups of Consciousness meditations via email one, three, or five times a week.

Or you can try the Tall Cups of Consciousness. Every three weeks I do a live online video energy session. The sessions are available as audio and video downloads after the live event.

Over the years I have recorded more than a thousand meditations and hundreds of online classes and topic-oriented energy healing sessions. You can pick and choose among the meditations, sessions, or classes that interest you. I also have many free meditations and Conscious Conversations available at aleyadao.com.

If you choose, I will continue to journey with you in the higher realms. Perhaps it will be in dreamtime or online, or maybe our paths will cross in the physical realm.

About the Author

*A*leya splits her time between Santa Barbara and the Sierra Nevada foothills north of Clovis, where she shares a home with her husband and her Akita-dalmatian, Freckles.

As a healer for more than twenty years, Aleya began her career at the age of twenty as a massage therapist and went on to get her master's degree in Oriental Medicine. She began the first alternative healing clinic in Telluride, Colorado, The Healing Company. She moved to California in 2004 and opened her healing doors in Santa Barbara and online. In 2009 she began delivering her audio and video Cups of Consciousness meditations to subscribers all over the world.

When Aleya is not working with clients, recording meditations, or creating sound healing music, she spends time on the water with dolphins and whales; paddleboards; gardens; designs fairy compounds; and daydreams about her next creative endeavor.